Royal
CEREMONIES OF STATE

Royal CEREMONIES OF STATE

John Brooke-Little

Country Life Books

Published by Country Life Books
and distributed for them by
The Hamlyn Publishing Group Limited
London . New York . Sydney . Toronto
Astronaut House, Feltham, Middlesex, England

First published 1980

ISBN 0 600 37628 1

Designed and produced by
Adkinson Parrish Limited, London

Filmset in 'Monophoto' Sabon by
Servis Filmsetting Limited, Manchester

Printed and bound in Hong Kong by
Leefung-Asco Printers Limited

Contents

For my cousin,
Celia Thornton,
without the use of whose
library the compilation
of this book would
have been far more
laborious.

Preface

This book is a mixture of history and my personal experience as one involved in ceremonial. I have tried to write about what ceremony is and what it means; why I believe it to be important, indeed essential; and how ceremonies of state are arranged and executed. Although this is not a crusading book, I must confess to the hope that those who read it may begin to see in ceremonial more than the pageant, the tourist attraction and 'the thing we British do so well'; that they may see in ceremonial a defence against chaos and anarchy, and so become its protagonists for that reason above all others.

The main purpose of this preface is to acknowledge the help I have received from various people while writing the book. My brother Officers of Arms, both South and North of the border, have been most helpful on the many occasions when I have essayed to 'pick their brains'; I am most grateful. I am indebted to various departments of the Royal Household, especially Mrs Wall of the Press Office at Buckingham Palace, for their sound advice and valuable suggestions.

I would particularly like to thank my clerk for over twenty years (which seems a rather unchivalrous remark, but I know I shall be forgiven), Miss Mary Rose Rogers, who not only typed my hieroglyphic manuscript and made useful suggestions, but also coped with the problems engendered by an absentee boss. During my absence, I was, of course, at home working on the book in the bosom of my long-suffering family. Lastly, therefore, my thanks to them for their patience and forbearance.

J.B. Brooke-Little
Richmond

Foreword

One of the earliest occasions of ceremony that I can recall is the time, as a small boy dressed in a sailor suit, I was taken to see a parade of Sea Cadets. It was still the fashion in the 1920s for small boys to wear sailor suits, so the national ritual was complete. I enjoyed the spectacle of uniforms, bugles, cymbals and the marching drum-beat to the extent of wanting to take part, and I believe it is this kind of feeling that lies at the heart of ceremonies: there is something about such an occasion which draws everyone concerned closer together. Hence the uplifting of the spirit and a significance beyond the rational.

Her Majesty the Queen said in her broadcast after her coronation in 1953: 'The ceremonies you have seen today are ancient, and some of their origins are veiled in the mists of the past. But their spirit and their meaning shine through the ages, never, perhaps, more brightly than now'. The need for formalized conduct lies deep in the human subconscious, whether it is expressed in the bosom of the family, in a gathering of friends, or in the expression of national emotions.

John Brooke-Little, Richmond Herald, has been my companion in arms for thirty years. His experience of ceremonies and his understanding as an historian will explain how it is that in Great Britain we have a reputation for ordering these matters well.

The College of Arms, A. Colin Cole, Esquire,
Queen Victoria Street, C.V.O., T.D., F.S.A.
London, E.C.4. Garter Principal King of Arms.

Chapter 1

Ceremony

One of the meanings ascribed to the word 'ceremony' in the *Shorter Oxford English Dictionary* is 'an empty form'. Another meaning, 'pomp, state', is perhaps not so 'archaic' as the compilers believed; for many people think of ceremony as being empty and pompous, something which has, or should have, no place in the modern, no-nonsense, bustling, utilitarian world.

In fact, ceremony is and always has been part of everyone's way of life. It is essentially a symbolic way of marking an event; a tidy and ordered way of doing things; an extension of conventional manners. When I think of ceremony there always comes to my mind Maurice Hare's limerick:

> There once was a man who said 'Damn!
> It is borne in on me what I am
> An engine that moves
> In predestinate grooves,
> I'm not even a bus, I'm a tram'.

Ceremony is like a tram. It moves in predestinate grooves and does not career across the road of life causing havoc and misery. It keeps to the rails, which are the rules of civilized behaviour.

Ceremonies mark the passage through life of individuals and families and the passage through the centuries of groups of people, institutions and nations. Individuals observe such small ceremonies as shaking hands when they meet, nice old-fashioned gentlemen first removing the right glove to show that no weapon is being concealed. A man, if he has been properly brought up, removes his hat when he meets a lady, opens the door for others, eats in a way which will not put others off their food; in short, he bears in mind the famous motto of William of Wykeham's two foundations – Winchester College and New College, Oxford – 'Manners makyth man'. Actually, the converse is really the case – man makyth manners, but

he does so for the best of reasons: ordered, tidy and elegant living.

Families too observe ceremonies. Before a meal the members of a Christian family bow their heads and someone says grace or, as the Americans have it – and in America the custom is more honoured than it is in Britain today – asks a blessing. Grace was the first ceremony in which I remember participating. It was a custom of the family with whom I was staying, when just three years old, for the youngest bachelor to say grace. The head of the family, who really should have had more sense, called on me. All I knew about grace was that it was my nanny's name, so I stood on my chair and shouted 'Gracie!'. The company was curiously unamused.

Birthdays, silver weddings and other such events are normally celebrated by the family with some ceremony, even if it is just the ceremony of blowing out the candles and cutting the cake.

Groups of people and organizations indulge in more elaborate ceremonies which often not only mark an important occasion but provide that continuity, without which people tend to feel insecure. Many towns still have a mayor-making ceremony at which the new mayor, resplendent in robes of office, is formally installed as the chief citizen of the town. About his neck is placed the mayoral chain and badge and he is preceded by an official bearing the civic mace, symbol of the royal authority and in some places also a sword, symbolizing justice. For one year the mayor will represent the town. In him it will be personified and it is therefore fitting that he should be seen to be a person set apart, not to build up his own ego but to maintain the dignity of the corporation which he heads.

While most towns have some sort of mayor-making ceremony, that of the City of London is by far

The Lord Mayor in his coach, with an escort of Pikemen from the Honourable Artillery Company, passing the Mansion House on Lord Mayor's Day, 1971.

the grandest and most spectacular. The Lord Mayor is not simply the first citizen of one of the greatest cities of the world, he is the embodiment of civic pride and dignity and his official journeys abroad, which are now customary, are almost regal in their splendour; they are also extremely popular and do a great deal for the prestige of both the City and the country.

The Lord Mayor's Show, which takes place on the Saturday nearest to 9 November, has become a national event. People flock to London to witness the colourful and seemingly endless procession of floats and bands, soldiers and carriages, which winds its way through the City. But perhaps they sometimes forget that the pageant which they are enjoying, although like all pageants it is in the nature of a ceremony, exists not just for the purpose of honouring the new Lord Mayor and brightening an often cold and gloomy November day, it has a more serious purpose. The Lord Mayor goes in state from the Mansion House to the Law Courts in the Strand to be presented to Her Majesty's Judges, and to receive the Sovereign's approval of his election, conveyed by the Lord Chancellor. This is the real reason for the procession; it is not so much a show as a solemn ceremony but, like so many ceremonies, it is accompanied by light-hearted and jubilant celebration.

If I were asked to name the elements which are the main constituents of solemn ceremonies, other than prescribed and traditional ritual, I think I would plump for procession, vesture and the use of symbolic objects. I have mentioned mayoral robes, badges and maces, and processions through the streets but there are many other such occasions in other different walks of life. The solemnity attendant upon legal proceedings springs readily to mind. The judge's authority, dignity and, to some extent, anonymity are symbolized by his robes and wig. He sits beneath the representation of the royal coat of arms, signifying that he is the Queen's Judge, dispensing the royal and impartial justice. Counsel too are robed and wigged and the ushers of the court are in black gowns, thus giving to proceedings which can be awesome and emotional, a quiet and proper dignity. Before the Crown Courts are held, or on some convenient day early in the proceedings, the judges process in state to an appointed church, robed and accompanied by the High Sheriff of the county who is attired in uniform, or court dress, together with other legal officials and often also by the Mayor and corporation of the town where the court sits. There a service is held to invoke God's help in the administration of justice. 'Give wisdom, O Lord, we pray Thee, to all those who are concerned in the administration of Thy Laws of Truth and Justice. . . .' So starts one of the collects. After the service, at which the High Sheriff's chaplain normally preaches the sermon, the judges proceed to the courts where they are sometimes met by a fanfare of trumpets from the High Sheriff's trumpeters, and the sitting of the court is formally opened. 'Sherriff' comes from the Old English 'Shire Reeve', the Crown's law-man; the modern High Sheriff is appointed by the Queen to serve for a year as her chief law-enforcement officer in that county. In practice the duties of the modern High Sheriff are mostly formal. He takes part in legal ceremonies, looks after the judges and undertakes a variety of social duties.

An even grander ceremony takes place in London to mark the beginning of the legal year which, like the academic year, begins in the Michaelmas term. On this occasion, the Lord Chancellor, with macer, purse-bearer and train-bearer, the Master of the Rolls, the Lord Chief Justice and all the Judges, Queen's Counsel and other barristers attend either a service at Westminster Abbey, or, if they are Roman Catholics, a Votive Mass of the Holy Ghost at Westminster Cathedral. Thereafter, they process to the House of Lords where the Lord Chancellor entertains them to 'breakfast'. This over they move to the Law Courts, reform the procession, which then winds its way through the great hall to the Lord Chief Justice's Court where the new Judges are welcomed before taking their places on the Bench.

Robes, similar to those worn by lawyers, are also worn by academics. These can be seen in profusion on such occasions as the annual Encaenia at Oxford University. This is the commemoration of the University's founders and benefactors and the occasion on which famous people are recognized by having honorary degrees bestowed upon them. A procession is formed, led by the Chief Constable and University Marshal. The Chancellor, at present Mr Harold Macmillan, is frequently present in his splendid robes of black brocaded silk with gold trimmings and matching hat. Then come the Vice-Chancellor, the Heads of the Colleges, doctors and other alumni of the University, mostly robed in scarlet and black,

and wearing a great variety of academic hoods, the material and colour combining to proclaim the wearer's degree. The procession makes its way to the Sheldonian Theatre, Sir Christopher Wren's curious masterpiece, where many University ceremonies are held. The Chancellor takes his place on his elaborate throne and the assembled company listens to the Public Orator extolling the benefactions and merits of those who are about to be honoured. This he still does in Latin, the universal language of scholarship, which may not give many of those present an intellectual feast, but they cannot but admire the sound of a great and lyrical language, eloquently declaimed.

This ceremony is far more staid than it used to be, for there was a time when there was much merry-making at the Encaenia, the proceedings being lightened by the frivolities of a buffoon, known as *Terrae Filius* ('son of the earth'). John Evelyn records in his diary that at the Encaenia held in June 1669 to celebrate the opening of the Sheldonian, *Terrae Filius*, (the University Buffoon) 'entertained the auditory with a tedious, abusive, sarcastical rhapsody, most unbecoming the gravity of the University, and that so grossly, that unless it be suppressed, it will be of ill consequence, as I afterwards plainly expressed my sense of it both to the Vice-Chancellor and several Heads of Houses, who were perfectly ashamed of it . . . in my life, I was never witness to so shameful entertainment'. So perhaps it is as well that solemnity has returned to an occasion where one of the noblest and most ancient universities of the world honours the great men of the world.

Processions and robes, enriched by ritualism, liturgy, symbolism and mysticism, find their apotheosis in man's worship of God. At the basis of most forms of worship is sacrifice. Primitive man knew only one way of appeasing his gods and that was by offering sacrifice. Special people were set apart to offer sacrifices, which were made in a solemn and ceremonial way lest the deities, instead of being appeased, might feel mocked. A god believed to be omnipotent, must be treated with respect, that is with good manners, which is ceremony. Whether the sacrifice was intended to curry favour, express gratitude, expiate offence, or avert the arbitrary wrath of a capricious deity, it had to be excellent and perfectly offered.

Many gods demanded human sacrifices, which were not just confined to primitive tribes, being widely practised by the Phoenicians and even by the Greeks and Romans. The Jews had and have elaborate sacrificial ceremonies as a glance at the book of Leviticus makes abundantly clear and, even today, sacrifice still forms an important, if not the central theme of worship in the great religions of the world. The Roman, Greek and High Anglican Churches all offer the sacrifice of the body and blood of Christ in the form of bread and wine. Buddhists offer first fruits and flowers and Mohammedans alms. Evangelicals and non-conformists, although admitting of no sacrifice, believe in alms giving and personal sacrifice to make them worthy to approach God. Naturally, it is in those religions where formal sacrifice is still practised that the most elaborate rituals and ceremonies take place, but acts of public worship in almost all religions are performed ceremonially. From a simple baptism in a village church to a solemn High Mass in a great cathedral, the elements I have detailed are present. At a baptism, the minister is vested in cassock, surplice and tippet. There is often a procession from the altar to the font where the symbolic element of water is used, along with words and actions prescribed by the rubrics. A sacrament is administered and the outward sign of this inward grace is to be found in the ceremonial forms used. It is

the same at a wedding. Bride and groom wear special clothes, the minister is vested, the wedding party processes down the nave to the altar where certain words are said and, as a symbol of what is happening, rings are exchanged or a single ring is placed on the bride's finger.

From such simple ceremonies, it is but a logical step to the magnificence of a *missa solemnis* where priests clad in symbolic vestments go through the ritual movements of the bloodless sacrifice, swathed in the odour of incense and to the sound of solemn music, handling with reverence the sacred and symbolic vessels.

Recently the ceremonies of the Roman Church have been simplified by the Sacred Congregation of Rites, because it is possible, and this is a danger inherent in all ceremonial, to pay too much attention to the outward signs and not enough to what is really happening. However, that having been said, the intention of the Sacred Congregation was not to abolish the age-old ceremonies of the Church. As the

Priests concelebrating High Mass.

Instruction on the Sacred Liturgy states 'it must be clearly understood that the aim of the Second Vatican Council's Constitution on the Sacred Liturgy is not simply to bring about changes in the liturgical forms and texts but rather to give inspiration and encouragement to that instruction of the faithful and that pastoral activity which has the Liturgy for its source and finds in the Liturgy the height of its expression'.

If I have seemed to lay emphasis on the liturgy of the Roman Catholic Church, this has been done for a purpose. The Roman Catholic Church is, in a sense, the mother of all Christian churches and in many of those which have broken away from it and later possibly from each other, some beliefs and some

vestiges of ceremony and forms of worship are still discernible.

This is particularly true of the Established Church of England and it is with ceremonies connected with this Church and with the Sovereign as its Supreme Governor that this book is principally concerned. The greatest ceremony that takes place in the British Commonwealth is the coronation of a sovereign and this ceremony, more than any other, is based on precedents going back centuries before the Reformation.

Although many ceremonies owe part of their significance either to man's dependence on his god or gods, or to rulers of nations who are charged with the administration of divine laws, there is another sort of

ceremony which, for distinction, I shall call triumphal ceremony. I refer, in the main, to martial ceremonies; jingoistic ceremonies intended to rally, inspire and reassure the people; to make them feel proud of their country and ready to fight and die for it if necessary. Such ceremonies are really shows of strength and, like religious ceremonies, are as old as mankind. They are essentially emotive and ceremony, colour, ordered processing and music, whether the beat of tribal drums, the skirl of the pipes or massed bands playing 'Land of Hope and Glory', play their full part.

Such ceremonies are unashamed triumphalism, a word which comes from the Latin *triumphus*, meaning a triumphal procession. The *triumphi* of ancient Rome were accorded by the Senate and People of

Rome to victorious generals and may be regarded as the forerunners of European military processions.

On the day of the triumph the honoured general assembled his soldiers outside the city, addressed them in suitably commendatory terms and, more important from their point of view, distributed among them the spoils of the enemy. He was then driven to the triumphal gate, welcomed by the Senate and led along the *Via Sacra* to the Capitol. The procession must have resembled the Lord Mayor of London's procession, inasmuch as the hero, clad in a gold embroidered robe and flowered tunic, his brows encircled with laurel and holding a laurel bough and sceptre, rode in a circular chariot drawn by four horses. He was accompanied by the military, trumpeters and flute-players and by the equivalent of the floats in the Lord Mayor's Show, but in this case the captives, some of whom were destined to be sacrificed to Jupiter, and carriages piled with spoils of battle. It is not difficult to conjure up the scene. The heat and noise and dust; the half-tipsy crowd cheering and shouting; the flash of sun on armour; the triumphant general high above the crowds, godlike; the screams of the sacrificial victims – all these were very much part of the 'grandeur that was Rome'.

It has been but a short step from those Roman triumphs to the Field of the Cloth of Gold and then, spine-chillingly, to Hitler's awe-inspiring shows of strength and to the great military parade which takes place in Moscow each year, when monstrous engines of death are paraded through the streets.

We, in Britain, are not guiltless of such military displays, but ours are scarcely the sort which are likely to terrify potential enemies or give people confidence in our military might. Rather they play on the emotions, stiffening upper lips, making us proud to be British and giving all the spectators, whatever their nationality, goose pimples and a funny feeling in the pits of their stomachs.

Even in the depth of winter, traffic can find it difficult to circumnavigate the Victoria Memorial when the guard is being changed at Buckingham Palace and the Queen's Birthday Parade, better known as Trooping the Colour, gets top television ratings and, incidentally, also brings the capital to a standstill.

So what of ceremony in the future. Will it survive an age which is increasingly agnostic, materialistic and iconoclastic? Or has it had its day and will it only survive in those basic politenesses which make life tolerable?

A romantic conception of a Roman triumph painted by Peter Paul Rubens. The victorious general is shown in his chariot with some of the spoils of battle.

Henry VIII arriving at the Field of the Cloth of Gold. A painting after the original by Valpe.

I believe that ceremony is so ingrained in human nature that it will survive until the end of time. Old ceremonies may die, others may change but new ones will be born. This is history. Human sacrifices have had their day, at least I trust that such ceremonies are dead. The ceremonies of the Roman Church have been modified, but they have been changed not abolished. New ceremonies are constantly evolving.

Think of the football match. A hundred years ago football was an amusing pastime. Today, especially in the United States of America, it is a ritual. I recently attended the annual American football match between Virginia Military Institute and its dreaded rival Virginia Polytechnic Institute. I knew at once that I was in what the Americans might call 'a ceremony situation'. From all over the country alumni had gathered in their thousands in the carparks. Before the match began they tail-gated. That is, they parked

their automobiles and laid out feasts which made civic banquets look like mid-morning snacks. Hosts placed symbols on the roofs of their cars so as to rally their guests. I had to keep my eyes skinned for an 'Old-Timer sitting on the john'. He was very obvious: four feet of lurid plastic sculpture. The match itself was ritualistic to an extreme. Bands and military cadets marched and countermarched all over the pitch. Scantily clad female cheer-leaders did their best to incite the vast crowds to frenzy and the stray clowns reminded me forcefully of *Terrae Filius* and his medieval antecedents. Then came the contestants, clad like tournament knights in body armour and helmets, parading around the field of play. The game began and it was essentially ceremonious. Every few

Opposite: *William Bruges, the first Garter King of Arms, before St George, from* Bruges' Garter Book, *c.1430.*

seconds the teams took up their positions. They scuffled furiously, either losing or gaining ground and then started again. What had obviously originated as a rough and tumble game had become a tough but essentially decorous and ceremonial contest. It was rather like a ritual dance; it was twentieth century ceremony *par excellence*.

People have tried worshipping God informally and without any ceremony or order but it has never really worked. You cannot treat your superior as an equal, if only because he is not. So there is even now a return by the devotees of 'do it yourself' worship to a modest ritual.

Every nation has its ceremonial observances but in Great Britain ours are more elaborate, more colourful and so more popular than in almost any other country. They will survive if only for the worst possible reason – money. The splendour, dignity and antiquity of our State Ceremonies and the awe in which the Sovereign is held are great tourist attrac-tions. Like some vast screen epic, they earn the country millions of pounds each year. If political ideology ever triumphs over the shopkeeper mentality, it will indeed be a sad day because all that will happen is that money-spinning ceremonies will give way to dreary proletarian ceremonies; and, as they will still be ceremonies, albeit unproductive ones, no point will have been scored.

The only danger is, that while ceremonies of one sort and another are bound to continue as part of the pattern of life, some ancient ceremonies may be altered beyond recognition and so lose a valuable attribute – continuity. As I have mentioned, the re-enactment of a ceremony over the centuries gives people a sense of continuity and so of security. This, as long as it does not dissolve into complacency, must be good for the body politic. Obviously there will be, as there have always been, changes, but I sincerely hope that the great ceremonies, the predestinate grooves on which the tram of state runs so securely, will remain. Whether they do or not, some form of ceremony must continue to guide the lives of men; the alternative is chaos and anarchy.

Chapter 2

The Heralds

I have found that the average person, if such there be, is almost totally ignorant of what a herald is, or does. Among the *cognoscenti* it is a perennial joke that heralds are generally thought to be 'gentlemen of the press'. In fact, this mistake is by no means unknown. Some people, unable to believe that I am Richmond Herald, introduce me as 'from *The Richmond Herald*' and on two occasions I have been led to the seats reserved for the press at public meetings.

The minds of others are clouded by thoughts of Christmas cards adorned with Herald Angels and, quite rightly as it happens, connect heralds with proclaimers and messengers. Yet others, again correctly, see some connexion between heralds and heraldry, the study of coats of arms.

Those who know that there are still officers called heralds, who appear at great state ceremonies, may not know what these officers actually do, but they think they know how to recognize them by what they wear. The trouble is that the herald's tabard bears a superficial resemblance to the coat of a state trumpeter and also to that of a Yeoman of the Guard and a Yeoman Warder of the Tower, so even sartorially there is frequently confusion.

The truth of the matter is that heralds tend to live up to their corporate motto 'diligent and secret'. They undertake and have undertaken many and various tasks including the arrangement of and participation in state ceremonies, which is why I am devoting a chapter to the history of the ancient office of herald.

Although official references to heralds do not appear until the end of the thirteenth century, it can be inferred from some of these references that heralds must have been active since at least the end of the previous century. Sir Anthony Wagner in *Heralds of England* cites a charter dated 18 March 1276 in which reference is made to one Peter, king of heralds north of the river Trent. It therefore seems certain that by this date there were not only degrees of herald but that a king of heralds enjoyed some form of territorial jurisdiction. This in turn suggests that the office of herald must have been evolving for quite some time before 1276. This assumption is supported by references to heralds in much earlier French poems and romances.

These early heralds were essentially concerned with the organization of the tournament, the mock battle, which was originally a form of military training for the knights and nobles who could be described as the conscripted officers of feudal society. The heralds proclaimed the tournament, named and extolled the prowess of the combatants and encouraged them as they fought.

A poem in French, detailing a tournament which took place at Chauvency in 1285, recites that heralds are endowed with the ability to speak of arms (*entalenté a parler d'armes* – the motto of The Heraldry Society). This, however, raises the question, what are arms?

On King Richard I's second Great Seal, which was probably struck in 1194, the king is depicted in armour and on horseback, bearing a shield decorated with three lions one above the other. This is the first evidence of a king of England using a device which has been proudly borne by our sovereigns ever since. The king's adoption of the three lions typifies what was happening all over the country at the close of the twelfth century. Everywhere nobles and knights were adopting colourful, symbolic devices which they displayed on their shields, banners, seals and coat armour. The coat armour was a long sleeveless coat worn over the mail as an extra protection against sword blows to the body and it is because these personal devices were shown on the coat armour that

A herald reading the proclamation of the coronation of King George V at Charing Cross.

they came to be called coats of arms, or, more succinctly, arms. That the heralds knew all about coats of arms towards the end of the thirteenth century has always suggested to me that they were in on the act from the beginning. It has been shown that heralds, as tournament masters, were expected to be able to recognize the combatants. This cannot have been a simple task when those taking part came from all over the country, but it would have been much easier if everyone displayed a unique personal device.

We know, from the study of old seals, literary references and other sources, that it had long been customary to decorate shields, but such decoration does not appear to have been systematic. What emerged in the early thirteenth century was an ordered system of personal symbolism identifiable by certain important characteristics. Briefly those were as follows: the principal vehicle for the display of the devices was the shield, the devices being designed and ordered so as to fit its flat-iron shape; arms were essentially symbolic rather than representational and

their design followed certain conventions or rules aimed at making them distinct and easily recognizable from afar; they were hereditary in character, descending in much the same way as a surname, but because, to avoid confusion, no two people could bear exactly the same coat of arms, differences were added by cadets of the family to the arms of the head of the family; they were honourable in character because only the nobles and knights who needed to be recognized used shields, coat armour and seals; and finally, they were governed by law, so as to maintain their exclusive character and to protect each man's right to his own arms.

Now my question is, how could such a system of unique, ordered and, just as important, beautiful symbolism have just happened within a couple of generations, had it not been consciously and deliberately organized? And if the validity of this question be accepted, organized by whom? I can conceive of no logical answers to these questions other than that it must have been deliberately

Henry VIII jousting before Queen Catherine at a tournament held in 1511: from the Westminster Tournament Roll.

hastened and masterminded and furthermore that the only people who could possibly have done this were the heralds. They alone had the opportunity, the ability and the personal interest, so it is scarcely surprising that the term heraldry later came to be applied to the study of coats of arms; it had become the principal business of a herald.

In the early days of the tournament there were a great many heralds. Most of these were originally itinerant but the more important were permanently attached to the households of the sovereign and the nobility. The heralds were often confused with the minstrels, who wandered around the country telling of the tournaments and feats of arms, singing of great romances and reciting epic poems. However, as time passed and the heralds became more and more concerned with heraldry and the marshalling of the increasingly elaborate and more elegant tournaments, the two groups became ever more distinct, also there were other reasons for this happening.

Heralds had early been distinguished by wearing their masters' cast-off coat armour and from the reign of Edward III (1327–1377) they were further distinguished by being given distinctive names or titles and being admitted to their offices by a formal ceremony of creation. This ceremony, which included baptism and the taking of an oath, was discontinued in the early seventeenth century, but it should be noted that heralds have also been formally created by Letters Patent under the great Seal since the late fifteenth century. The following brief quotation from the Letters Patent creating me Richmond Herald in April 1967 will serve to illustrate the solemn and formal nature of a herald's appointment.

> Elizabeth the Second by the Grace of God of United Kingdom of Great Britain . . . to all to whom these Presents shall come Greeting Whereas the Office of one of our Heralds of Arms commonly called Richmond is become vacant . . . Know Ye therefore that We for divers good causes and considerations Us hereunto especially moving of Our especial Grace certain knowledge and mere motion have advanced made constituted ordained and created . . . Our trusty and well beloved John Philip Brooke Brooke-Little . . . one of our Heralds of Arms and have given him . . . that name commonly called RICHMOND and do . . . give and grant unto (him) . . . the style title liberties pre-eminences anciently accustomed and belonging and appertaining to such office To have enjoy occupy and exercise that Office . . . during his good behaviour in the said office Moreover we have given and granted . . . unto (him) . . . an annuity or yearly rent of seventeen pounds sixteen shillings of good and lawful money of Great Britain . . . to be paid quarterly . . . at the office of the Chamberlain of Our Household . . . Together with all fees rights perquisites privileges pre-eminences, advantages and emoluments whatsoever to the said Office incident or belonging . . . In Witness whereof We have caused these Our Letters to be made Patent . . . By Warrant under the Queen's Sign Manual.

I shall explain later how I and my brother heralds manage to survive on £17.80p *per annum*. In fact, this 'quaint mediaeval salary' as the press sometimes describes it, represents a reduction of the salary of £26. 13s. 4d (that is forty marks) granted to heralds in 1618, because William IV, in an effort to cut his household expenses, reduced all salaries in 1831.

From the beginning heralds had not been solely occupied as tournament marshals; they would have led the very idle life their detractors alleged they did if this had been the case. They filled in their time by acting as masters of ceremonies in their lords' house-

Four heralds in tabards and carrying wands of office: from the Westminster Tournament Roll.

holds and it is from this employment that the later concern of the royal heralds with ceremonies of state probably stems. As time went on the heralds were more and more employed as proclaimers, messengers and even ambassadors. They exercised their office not simply in tournaments and in peacetime, but also in battle. In Shakespeare's *King Henry V*, after the surrender of Harfleur, Charles VI of France says to his Constable

> Therefore, lord constable, haste Mountjoy
> And let him say to England that we send
> To know what willing ransom he will give.

Mountjoy, who is a French King of Heralds, rides to the English camp and addresses King Henry thus:

MOUNTJOY   You know me by my habit
KING   Well, then, I know thee: what shall I know of thee?
MOUNTJOY   My master's mind.
KING   Unfold it.
MOUNTJOY   Thus says my king. [Mountjoy then delivers his message and ends:] So far my king and master, so much my office.
KING   What is thy name? I know thy quality.
MOUNTJOY   Mountjoy.
KING   Thou dost thy office fairly. Turn thee back, And tell thy king . . .

Here we see a herald, wearing a tabard and so identifiable as a herald, bearing a special name or title by which he is addressed and acting, on the orders of the Constable of France, as a royal ambassador in time of war.

The connexion with warfare and the Constable is important. The early mediaeval royal household was divided into the courtyard, the hall and the chamber; respectively in the care of the Constable, the Steward

and the Chamberlain. The royal heralds, because of their association with matters military naturally came under the principal military officers of the realm as well as being courtiers. Later these great officers of state came to be called the Lord High Constable and the Earl Marshal and they presided over a court of law variously known as the *Curia Militaris*, Court of the Constable and Marshal, Court of Chivalry, or more recently Court of the Earl Marshal. Mr G.D. Squibb Q.C., an eminent authority on the history of the Court of Chivalry (which is its most usual name and therefore the one by which I shall hereinafter refer to it), believes it was instituted in 1347–8 to have cognizance of certain causes. There is no need to delve here into the complex history of the Court and of the various causes over which, from time to time, it had jurisdiction. Suffice it to say that after the execution of Edward Stafford, Duke of Buckingham and Lord High Constable of England, in 1531 the office of Constable was not revived, except for ceremonial purposes on the day of a coronation. The Earl Marshal therefore became the sole hereditary judge in the Court of Chivalry, which today still has jurisdiction over matters relating to the bearing of coats of arms. He also became solely responsible for the preparation of ceremonies of state and for the royal heralds who act as his staff officers on these occasions. Since 1672 the Earl Marshalship has been vested in the holder of the Dukedom of Norfolk, the premier dukedom of England. The present holder of the office is Major-General Miles Francis (Fitzalan-Howard) 17th Duke of Norfolk, Earl of Arundel, Earl of Surrey, Earl of Norfolk, Baron Fitzalan, Clun and Oswaldestre, Baron Beaumont, Baron Maltravers and Baron Howard of Glossop, C.B., C.B.E., M.C.

I now revert to the heralds: I have mentioned that,

A drawing by Sir Peter Lely of two heralds (c. 1670) wearing tabards of the Stuart Royal Arms.

particular. It is loosely used to describe kings, heralds and pursuivants of arms in general, as well as the middle rank in particular. Up to now I have used it in its widest sense so as not to confuse the issue, but, strictly speaking, it is better to use the expression 'officers of arms' as the generic term.

There was not enough work for the bands of wandering heralds, as their numbers seem to have decreased as the centuries passed and more and more heralds and pursuivants became attached to the households of the greater nobility. In the royal household there were also kings of arms as well as various heralds and pursuivants. These may once have worn their royal master's cast-off coat armour but royal accounts show that coats had to be provided for the royal officers. The original long coat armour worn by the Normans gradually became shorter and eventually developed by the fourteenth century into the tight-fitting jupon. This, in turn, gave way in the mid-fifteenth century to a more elaborate garment, called a tabard. This resembled two playing-cards joined at the shoulders, each emblazoned with the owner's arms, while smaller panels, similarly decorated, formed the sleeves. Although tabards were not worn after the end of the fifteenth century, the royal officers of arms continued to wear tabards of the royal arms and this they still do. Today all tabards are embroidered, those of the kings of arms on velvet, of the heralds on satin and of the pursuivants on damask silk. Tabards were once worn over ordinary dress but a military style uniform was introduced in 1831, which underwent various alterations, but officers of arms now wear black knee breeches with silk stockings (alas, now heavy-duty nylon tights) and buckled shoes. Their tunics are of scarlet cloth, embroidered, according to rank, with varying amounts of incredibly expensive gold lace. Court swords are worn and cocked hats with ostrich feathers, cloaks or greatcoats.

In the fifteenth century the struggle between the Crown and the nobility came to a head. The nobles sought to aggrandize themselves by every means in their power. They fortified their houses, issued liveries to vast numbers of servants, including, of course, their heralds and pursuivants, and, by a display of armed power, essayed to impress and overawe their rivals and give the king himself every reason to feel uneasy and every cause to seek ways in which to limit and control the dangerous pretentions of the nobility.

This struggle for power virtually ceased after the Battle of Bosworth Field in 1485. Henry VII ascended the throne and determined to rule in his own way. Laws against subjects maintaining liveried retainers were passed but it was not so much the law as the state

at a fairly early date, there emerged two degrees of herald – heralds and kings of heralds, the latter having some sort of territorial jurisdiction. As heralds were also called heralds of arms, kings of heralds were known as kings of heralds of arms, which was a bit of a mouthful, so they came to be known simply as kings of arms. Later, apprentices were appointed and these were known as pursuivants (usually pronounced 'persevants'). At first they wore no coat of arms but later we find them being formally created like heralds, being given names or titles and wearing their master's coat, albeit often athwart (that is with the sleeves over the front and back) to demonstrate that they were not fully-fledged heralds. What makes everything rather confusing is that the term herald is both generic and

Four heralds photographed outside the College of Arms in 1969 demonstrating four versions of official uniform.

of the realm that enabled Henry to achieve a bloodless victory. The nobility were relatively impoverished after years of civil strife, many great houses had become extinct and the Renaissance and a less feudal attitude to life was everywhere beginning to make itself felt. It is not therefore surprising that private heralds and pursuivants, together with other liveried retainers, faded from the scene: the royal officers of arms alone remained.

By the end of the fifteenth century the heraldic duties and activities of the officers of arms are reasonably clearly defined. A king of arms called Norroy had amorial jurisdiction north of the river Trent and one called Clarenceux south of it. There was sometimes also a king of arms with authority in

Wales. There was a senior king, first created by King Henry V in 1415, called Garter King of Arms. He was the senior herald of all England but did not have jurisdiction over a province. The practice of the kings of arms of granting arms to worthy men and corporations, such as trade guilds, towns, colleges and the like was becoming well established and they appear also to have been making heraldic visitations within their provinces. There were about a dozen principal heralds and pursuivants and doubtless other lesser fry. Naturally these officers kept books and records of arms and of other matters concerning their various duties. It is not surprising that they, like those who practised other crafts and mysteries, should have wished to be incorporated and granted a residence where they could maintain a library and more efficiently pursue their calling.

Richard III granted them their wish and by a charter dated 2 March 1484 he made Garter, Clarenceux, Norroy and Gloucester Kings of Arms and all other heralds and pursuivants and their successors in office a body corporate with perpetual succession. He also gave them a messuage called Coldharbour, which was a palatial house, the great hall of which overlooked the river and which boasted about forty rooms, together with stables, a lodge and various gardens. Unhappily the new owners had not even time to put the house in reasonable order before it was taken from them by Henry VII and given to his mother, the formidable Margaret, Countess of Derby. Whether the poor heralds' charter was quashed by King Henry is uncertain but there is no doubt that they were homeless until, in 1555, King Philip and Queen Mary gave them a house called Derby House just south of St Paul's. This was granted in a new charter which also reincorporated the officers by their titles, namely, Garter, Clarenceux and Norroy Kings of Arms, Richmond, Somerset, York, Lancaster, Windsor and Chester Heralds, and Portcullis, Rouge Croix, Rouge Dragon and Bluemantle Pursuivants. They and their successors in those offices became the corporate body soon to be known familiarly as the College of Arms of Heralds' College. Derby House was destroyed in the Great Fire of 1666 and the present building, now entered from Queen Victoria Street, was erected on the site.

There are no longer tournaments for heralds to marshal and proclaim; messages are passed by satellite in peace and war; a complex diplomatic corps has taken over the heralds' ambassadorial functions but the royal officers of arms still assist the Earl Marshal in the organization of ceremonies of state. They still attend the Sovereign in their splendid tabards; they design and the Kings of Arms grant, by the royal authority vested in them, new coats of arms to people and corporations of eminence throughout the Commonwealth; they maintain and interpret the official heraldic and genealogical records and advise the public on any matters concerning arms, pedigrees,

A grant of armorial bearings made in 1612 to William Lambart by William Camden, Clarenceux King of Arms.

ceremonial, precedence, chivalry and kindred subjects. For doing this they are allowed to charge professional fees and they also retain a portion of the official fees payable on grants of arms. This is why their salaries have remained unchanged and also why they are no charge on the Exchequer.

One of the officers, known as the Officer in Waiting, is on duty each day between 10 a.m. and 4 p.m., Monday to Friday and he will receive callers and answer queries addressed to the college by post or telephone. If he undertakes any work on someone's behalf, he will charge an appropriate fee and that person will become his personal, private client. For all practical purposes it is best to think of the college not as a firm, but as an address. The officers govern the College but they are not partners in a business. They are independent practitioners in heraldry and allied disciplines but in their ceremonial role they are servants of the Crown, responsible to the Earl Marshal of England.

Chapter 3

Monarchy

The expression 'constitutional monarchy' has been much used in this century, but it has been defined in a variety of ways, so making definition itself indefinite. I believe that Professor Charles Oman, sometime Chichele Professor of English History at Oxford University, summed up what it ought really to mean when he wrote 'the word constitution in all times, early and late, save when a fixed framework of laws exists to define the polity of a state' (as for example, in the United States of America) 'means little more than "habitual, and generally accepted by the nation".' If this definition is admissable, then the constitutional monarchy we enjoy in Britain is very different from that found in Norway, Sweden, Spain, or any other European country.

Our monarch is not just a figure-head with no real power; a sort of ventriloquist's dummy manoeuvered by a political party during its pleasure. What is 'habitual, and generally accepted by the nation' is a monarchy which is part of an enduring tradition, having evolved over many centuries. It has not been introduced by politicians and its powers, or lack of them, are not written into a fixed constitution. The rights of the Crown are known and can be detailed without difficulty. What is less simple is to evaluate the practical use of the Crown and to state at any one moment which of the Crown's privileges should be 'more honour'd in the breach than the observance'.

'Constitutional monarchy' has undertones of drabness about it which are scarcely in keeping with our own monarchy. For this reason, and also because of confusing the British monarchy with any other constitutional monarchy, I prefer to describe it as a ceremonial monarchy. That is a monarchy where all important constitutional actions are still performed in a traditional, formal and ceremonial manner; clinging to forms which may seem anachronistic but which,

because they are safe and chauvinistically British, are acceptable to the majority.

In a way, the British Constitution, if looked at objectively and critically by a foreigner, must seem not just anachronistic, but positively ridiculous. The House of Commons, that bastion of democracy, 'Mother of Parliaments' and guardian of Magna Carta, is a collection of representatives of geographical areas, because that is how it all began. In many cases the inhabitants of these areas now have little in common, yet the system has not adapted itself nor been adapted to industry and urbanization. We therefore have such curious situations as that which occurred after the October 1974 General Election. On this occasion the Labour Party polled 39.3 per cent of all votes cast and won 319 seats; the Conservatives polled 35.9 per cent and won 276 seats; the Liberals polled 18.3 per cent and won 11 seats, and other parties polled 6.4 per cent and won 26 seats. Now if we had had proportional representation Labour should have had about 248 seats, the Conservatives 227, and Liberals 115 and the other parties 40.

The House of Lords, although it has undergone three more or less dramatic constitutional changes during the course of this century, is still one of the oldest legislative chambers in the world. Its powers were first seriously pruned by the Parliament Act of 1911. This Act, brought in ostensibly because the Lords threw out Lloyd-George's swingeing Budget of 1909, but more particularly to stop them treating a Home Rule Bill for Ireland in the same cavalier way, had the effect of abolishing the right of the Lords to veto a Bill absolutely; in future their veto was to be suspensive, simply delaying a Bill for two years, a period later reduced to one year, or in the case of a Bill designated by the Speaker of the Commons as a Money Bill, one month. Had the Lords not passed this

28

self-mutilating legislation the King, George V, had agreed, albeit unwillingly, to create enough new hereditary peers to swamp the Lords with pro-Government votes. The same tactics had been used in 1832 in order to ensure the passing of the Reform Bill. There was no intention here to tamper with the Constitution but had the Tory peers continued to block the passage of the Bill, King William IV was prepared to create sufficient new peers to support Lord Grey, the protagonist of the Bill.

The second major constitutional change was the passing of the Act in 1958 enabling the Crown (some would argue that no enabling Act was required) to create Life Peerages for men and women, the women so created also being entitled to sit and vote in the Lords. Until the passing of this Act no peeress had been entitled to this privilege. At first the Act seemed to some but a minor change in the constitution of the House of Lords, for since 1876 the Crown had conferred Life Peerages on eminent judges, the Lords of Appeal in Ordinary. It was not then appreciated to what extent and in what ways successive Prime Ministers would advise the Crown to exercise this extension of the Royal Prerogative. In the event about 300 Life Peerages have been created between the passing of the Act and March 1979. In January 1979 the House of Lords was composed of three peers of the blood royal, two archbishops, twenty-five dukes, thirty marquesses, 159 viscounts, twenty-four bishops and 810 barons and baronesses. There are also seventy-three Irish peers who used to elect twenty-eight of their number to sit in the House of Lords, but no elections have been held since 1920. The Earl of Kilmorey, the last Irish representative peer, died in 1961.

The last Act which profoundly altered the Constitution and affected the House of Lords was the Peerage Act 1963. This Act gave all Scottish peers a right to a seat in the Lords, whereas before they had elected sixteen of their number to sit. It also gave seats to hereditary peeresses in their own right (that is not wives of peers, but actual holders of peerages). But as these were minor alterations in the constitution of the House, they did not greatly alter the Constitution of the Realm. No, the great constitutional innovation was that under the Act a hereditary peer was able, within one year of succeeding to a peerage, or if under twenty-one years of age, within one year of attaining that age, to disclaim it for the period of his life and so be eligible to vote in Parliamentary elections and to become a member of the House of Commons. However, although this Act is of profound constitutional significance, in the event very few have taken advantage of it. It enabled Viscount Stansgate, the Earl of Home and Viscount Hailsham to stand for election to the House of Commons which they entered as Mr A. Wedgwood-Benn, Sir Alec Douglas-Home and Mr Quintin Hogg. Now, ironically, the last two are back in the House of Lords as Life Peers. So far only fifteen peers have 'disclaimed'.

Then we come to the Crown itself. Under the Constitution the Crown is the ultimate source of power. The Sovereign makes peace and war, appoints ambassadors, judges and, as Commander in Chief of the Armed Forces, the officers thereof. The Crown is the Fount of Honour and so creates peers and confers honours. It is the Sovereign who summons, prorogues and dissolves Parliament and appoints and dismisses Ministers, including and more especially the Prime Minister. The Sovereign may veto Bills passed by both Houses of Parliament, which technically cannot become law without the royal assent. The Sovereign is also Supreme Governor of the Church of England and swears, as part of the Coronation Oath, to 'maintain the laws of God, the true profession of the Gospel and the Protestant reformed religion established by law'. The Sovereign appoints the archbishops and bishops, twenty-six of whom sit in the House of Lords. The Church of England is part of the Constitution.

In fact, as everyone knows, the Crown does not exercise any of these autocratic powers except upon the advice of its responsible Ministers. Even bishops are appointed on the advice of the Prime Minister. Constitutional historians tend to make much of the one power still sometimes exercised by the Sovereign, namely that of choosing the Prime Minister when there is no obvious candidate for the office, that is, where the governing party has no recognized leader or where no one party has an overall majority in the House of Commons. The latter situation could still arise and the Queen might be faced with having to ask various people, the accepted leaders of their parties, to try and form a Government. But the former situation, that of a party with no accepted leader, should not occur in future as the major political parties now have systems for electing party leaders. It is sometimes said that the Queen had to exercise this particular facet of her prerogative when Sir Anthony Eden was forced to resign the premiership in January 1957 and that she chose Mr Harold Macmillan. It is of course true that she made this choice, but it was on the advice of the late Lord Salisbury who, in turn, took soundings from the entire Cabinet. It was really a Cabinet decision and not a royal one, nor even, as Salisbury's critics

have hinted, a bit of king-making by Salisbury.

So what have we? An infinitely powerful Sovereign with virtually no personal power; a House of Lords with vestigial powers, many of whose members are there because they have succeeded to a hereditary dignity and suffer from the disqualification of neither bankruptcy nor insanity; a steadily increasing number of Life Peers, some created because of merit, some to remove them from the active political scene and some because of a patronage exercise by the Prime Minister which, had it been exercised by the Sovereign, would have been hotly criticized; and a group of bishops of the Church of England, whose communicating members represent about $3\frac{1}{2}$ per cent of the total population of the United Kingdom. Finally, there is the principal legislative assembly, the House of Commons, the ruling party in which is unlikely ever to represent the political wishes of more than a third of the enfranchised population.

The way I have described the Constitution makes *Alice in Wonderland* seem like a reasonable exposition of everyday life. I have done this deliberately because, if the facts are not faced, any apology for the Constitution is in danger of becoming sentimental.

Mercifully my apology is brief. It is simply this. Because Crown, Lords and Commons have evolved and adapted themselves to change over the centuries, because they provide continuity and hence stability of government, and because of a system of checks and balances provided by that most powerful force of all, public opinion, the system works, and works far better for Britain, and I stress *for Britain*, than any other system. Foreigners either look objectively and critically at our Constitution as I, acting as the devil's advocate, have attempted to do, and pronounce it mediaeval, politically indefensible and hence immoral, or else they go crazy about our quaint tradition and ceremonies and think that our monarchy is just too adorable and wonderful – for all the wrong reasons. The British like things the way they are and they do not feel oppressed; they see no point in change for the sake of change; they like foreigners to like their Queen and do not care a tinker's cuss if they think our institutions zany.

But there is a danger, a growing and very real danger. There are more and more people who wish to introduce change, not because it is needed, or wanted, but for ideological motives. They are not content for the Constitution to evolve slowly and after mature deliberation; they must be two jumps ahead. They are not content to rely on the good sense of the British people to provide the checks and balances, thus seeing that power is not abused; they must undermine the Constitution so as to change it completely. Let me quote two examples.

In the Commons the thin end of the wedge of 'Government by Referendum' has been recently introduced by holding the Common Market and Devolution referenda. This was not a natural evolution of the Constitution: it was simply a piece of political gerrymandering. The other example is that in the Lords the introduction of Life peerages, the cessation of the creation of hereditary peerages and plans by the two major parties to abolish or totally to reform the Lords do not seem to have sprung from any popular demand; the Lords, in its emasculated state, cannot interfere with the process of legislation and it has not, as it sometimes has in the past, attracted any particular odium. On the contrary its deliberations are generally considered more objective, thoughtful and constructive than those of the lower House.

The position of the Crown has not been directly challenged. This is probably because the head which wears it is that of a woman who is beloved and respected as a person and it is probably safe to say that as long as the Queen sits on the throne the monarchy is safe. The powers of the Queen cannot be eroded for she reigns as a responsible constitutional monarch. This means that the only way in which the monarchy, as an institution, can be diminished is as a ceremonial monarchy. Reduce the splendour of monarchy and the importance of ceremonial and tradition and the light of the Sovereign will gradually become dimmer and dimmer until snuffing it out will seem but the final act in a natural regression. The ideological critics of monarchy maintain a fairly low profile but they are there, anxious to bring about something which would not naturally happen. They criticize not the Sovereign but her advisers; not her way of life but the cost of maintaining it (the British are careful about money); not the hereditary nature of the monarchy but that of the House of Lords and so the hereditary principle.

I believe that the future of the monarchy rests in it being a ceremonial monarchy and a family monarchy and I believe it can continue to fulfil these rather different roles as efficiently and effectively as any family in the land combines formality with family life, as long as the British people look over their shoulders and recognize the enemies of the system, recalling perhaps the words of St Peter in the fifth chapter of his first Epistle 'Be sober, be vigilant, because your adversary the devil, as a roaring lion, walketh about, seeking whom he may devour: Whom resist steadfast in the faith'.

Opposite: Black Rod addressing the Speaker of the House of Commons, requesting the Commons presence at the bar of the Lords to hear the Queen's speech opening Parliament.

As I have asserted that changes in our curious system of government have been effected naturally and as I have defended the Constitution because it has evolved and adapted itself to circumstances rather than been forcibly altered, I must show, if only in a microcosmic way, how this has happened.

If this were a history book or a book on monarchy I would have had to start this narrative long before the Roman Conquest. But it is not, so I shall simply start at the moment when William of Normandy conquered England in 1066 and imposed upon the country a system of government known as the feudal system, from which our present Constitution has evolved. William rudely curtailed the gentle evolution of the English under their annointed kings, advised by their earls and prelates. He deposed their nobles, confiscated their estates and imposed an alien aristocracy and an alien system of government upon them. Far from bringing a European culture to the island nation, the Normans made England their milch-cow and dissipated the strength and resources of the country in interminable wars to satisfy their territorial ambitions in France; all, as it transpired after four hundred years of bloodshed, to no avail. England was a conquered nation and did not really emerge again as an island power until the advent of the Tudors in 1485. Not until then did the country regain its pride; it is a sobering thought.

The hereditary nature of the monarchy was established in pre-Norman times but not because there was anything sacrosanct in the hereditary principle; it was a matter of expediency. To avoid civil war every time the king died it was accepted that the choice of his successor should be confined to one of his near relatives. If the eldest son were a well-qualified person, he was to be preferred but essentially he was elected by the notables. Once elected, he was annointed by the priests, thus giving divine sanction to his election and according him a measure of heavenly protection. He was recognized and acclaimed by the people but this was an informal and popular recognition. Far more important and necessary was the fealty of the nobility which bound them to their chosen and annointed king. This has not changed. It is true that reference books now publish an 'order of succession to the throne' but this is only because the people have agreed that the strict hereditary system shall pertain, but only as long as this is the will of the people. The Sovereign is still annointed and still acclaimed at the Coronation and the Lords Spiritual and Temporal still do their fealty and homage. In this

A panel of the Wilton Diptych showing Richard II with Saints Edmund, Edward the Confessor and John the Baptist, being presented to the Blessed Virgin.

way, the mystique of sovereignty has been preserved.

For various reasons the order of succession has deviated from the direct line of descent over the centuries. At the very start of the Norman dispensation the Conqueror's eldest son Robert, because he was Duke of Normandy, did not succeed his father. His younger brother William became king and after him, his next brother Henry. Henry had no legitimate sons but his daughter Matilda had a son Henry who eventually became Henry II, but not before his cousin Stephen had reigned and Stephen's son William been passed over.

Richard II was succeeded by Henry IV who seized the throne and claimed it 'as by the right blood coming of King Henry (III)'. Not, be it noted, 'as by being nearest heir to our late cousin King Richard' but simply as being of the blood royal and so eligible for election and sacring.

The same is true of Henry VII who won the crown

from Richard III at Bosworth Field in 1485; he was not nearest in blood to the slain king. However, times were changing and more and more it was thought expedient to follow a definite line of succession, so Henry consolidated his claim by marrying Elizabeth, eldest daughter and co-heir of King Edward IV. During the Tudor dynasty which reigned from the accession of Henry VII until the death of Elizabeth in 1603, it was firmly established that a woman could succeed to the throne and that, where there were no sons, daughters were 'elected' in order of primogeniture. This is a fascinating sidelight on the legal history of the country when it is appreciated that, in the sixteenth century, women were in no way considered men's equals and possessed far fewer legal rights than were enjoyed by men. To state that they were their husbands' property is an over simplification, but it is not too far wide of the truth.

The order of succession, by now comfortably established as to be almost a constitutional necessity, was abruptly broken after the 'abdication by flight' of James II. The will of the people expressed through Parliament, diverted the succession. The election lighted not on James's son Charles, but upon his daughter Mary, who was to reign as joint Sovereign with her husband and cousin William of Orange. Indeed, the future succession was provided for by the Act of Settlement of 1701. By this Act, after William and Mary and their issue, Mary's sister Anne was to succeed, to be followed by her issue. Although she had many children none survived her, which meant that, under the terms of the Act, the throne was to pass to the nearest Protestant heir, Princess Sophia, Electress and Duchess Dowager of Hanover. In the event, the Electress died a few months before Queen Anne, so her son succeeded as George I in 1714. Thereafter the succession has continued uninterrupted save for the abdication of King Edward VIII.

No dictator, despot, or absolute monarch can rule for ever, unless he has the support of his subjects. You can suppress some of the people some of the time but not all the people all the time and wise rulers have appreciated this. The survival of the English monarchy has been due in great measure to the ability of the Sovereigns to delegate, compromise and carry the people with them.

As government became more complex, so the king was forced to delegate his powers. He needed money to manage the machinery of state, so he needed to woo those who paid the taxes which kept the country going. There had to be a *quid pro quo* if the king were

Opposite: *Part of a long printed roll published to commemorate the coronation of George IV in 1821.*

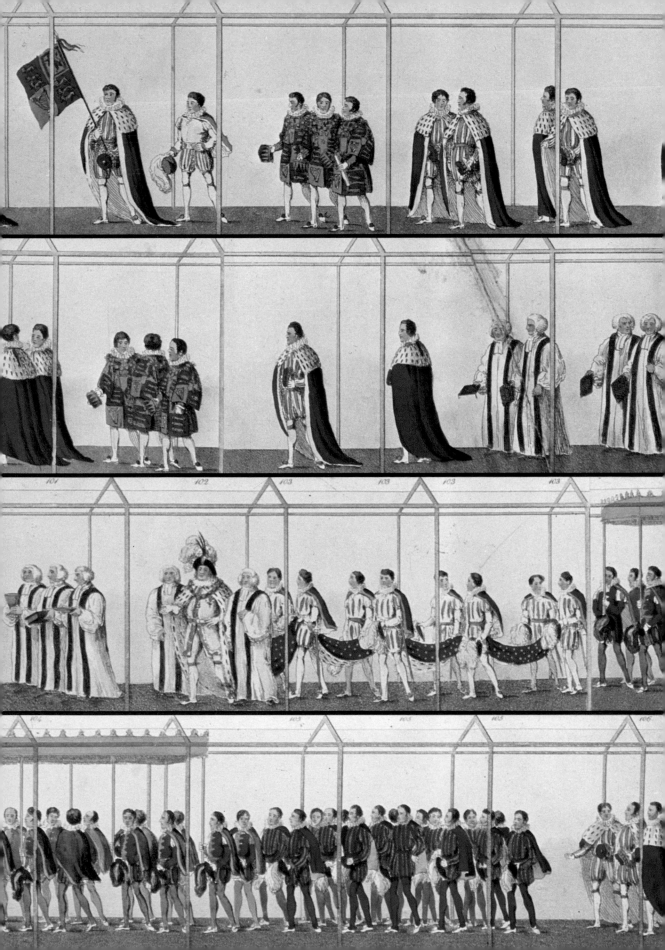

not to be dubbed a tyrannical extortionist and so be ripe for assassination. This was made quite clear at Runnymede in 1215, when King John was forced to accede to the demands of the nobles. In 1965 I and three other pursuivants accompanied Her Majesty when she went to St Paul's Cathedral to attend a service commemorating the 750th anniversary of the sealing of Magna Carta. This underlined the veneration for this particular document, which is often thought to have made all men free and guaranteed forever all the liberties of the English people. This is not quite true any more than is Sellar and Yeatman's evaluation of Magna Carta in *1066 and All That* where they state 'Magna Charter was therefore the chief cause of Democracy in England, and thus a *Good Thing* for everyone (except the Common People)'. The real value of this famous document lies in the fact that it sets down not a list of new freedoms but details the ancient liberties which John had violated. H.W.C. Davis in *England under the Normans and Angevins*, in some measure supports Sellar and Yeatman's lighthearted comment when he writes 'the rights of the lower classes receive much less attention and are less carefully defined than those of their superiors'. But whatever interpretation may be put on Magna Carta it made one thing clear and that is that the king must rule according to law. If he fails to do this his subjects are released from their allegiance.

Succeeding kings were forced more and more to honour this contract. Edward II and Richard II having been deemed to have acted outside the law were deposed and murdered, even though they were the Lord's annointed. James I believed in the divine right of kings and wrote that not only were they God's lieutenants upon earth, sitting on God's throne, but even by God himself were they called gods. For a subject to dispute what a king might do in the height of his power was sedition. James got away with it, but his luckless son, Charles I died upon the block and for the only time in its history England became a republic.

The history of constitutional monarchy really lies in the development of Parliament. From a body of nobles summoned from time to time to support and advise the king it became, as early as the thirteenth century, a representative body. The shires and towns were required to send representatives who increasingly augmented their power by granting the king money in return for promises of liberty and protection. It was really a sort of genteel blackmail.

Parliament executed Charles I and Parliament brought back Charles II. Parliament ordered the

Protestant succession so, when George I came to England, he was beholden to Parliament for his throne and in the main, was content to let his ministers govern the country, especially as he could not speak a word of English.

Somehow England managed to survive the reigns of the first four Georges and William IV. These monarchs seldom interfered with parliamentary government and when they did it was usually disastrous. They had no role to play other than to act as constitutional heads of state. They did nothing for the people, they set no example, except in loose living and extravagance (I except George III, who was mad, rather than bad) and they inspired no patriotism. The only reasons why they were tolerated were because it suited the politicians, because the memory of the Commonwealth was still green, and while the sovereigns did precious little good, they did no real harm and no one wanted a holocaust like the French Revolution in England.

It was during Queen Victoria's reign that the monarchy acquired a new dimension, the dimension that has ensured and I believe will continue to ensure its survival. In fact, it really had little to do with Victoria; it was her cousin and consort, Prince Albert of Saxe-Coburg Gotha, who fashioned modern constitutional ceremonial monarchy. The Queen and her family became the epitome of what a moral, respectable, God-fearing family should be. They attracted respect not odium. The Queen, though scarcely a genius, applied herself to the minutiae of government, insisting on being consulted and offering advice based, to a great extent, on the cautious wisdom of her husband. She performed the ceremonial acts of sovereignty in a dignified manner and so, although too partisan to be an ideal constitutional sovereign, laid the foundations for the role which future sovereigns would be required to fulfil.

In fact, she, or more accurately Prince Albert, fashioned a rod for her back, because when the Prince died the Queen was expected to continue to reign along the lines laid down so painstakingly by the Prince. She did no such thing. She refused to perform her public duties nursing her grief in widow's weeds at Balmoral or Osborne. She ignored all that her adored husband had taught her and when her unpopularity was so great as to constitute a real menace to the monarchy, she would not listen to the advice of Gladstone, her Prime Minister, that she should

Overleaf: *The Death Warrant of Charles I, 29 January 1648. The signature and seal of Oliver Cromwell are in the first column of signatories.*

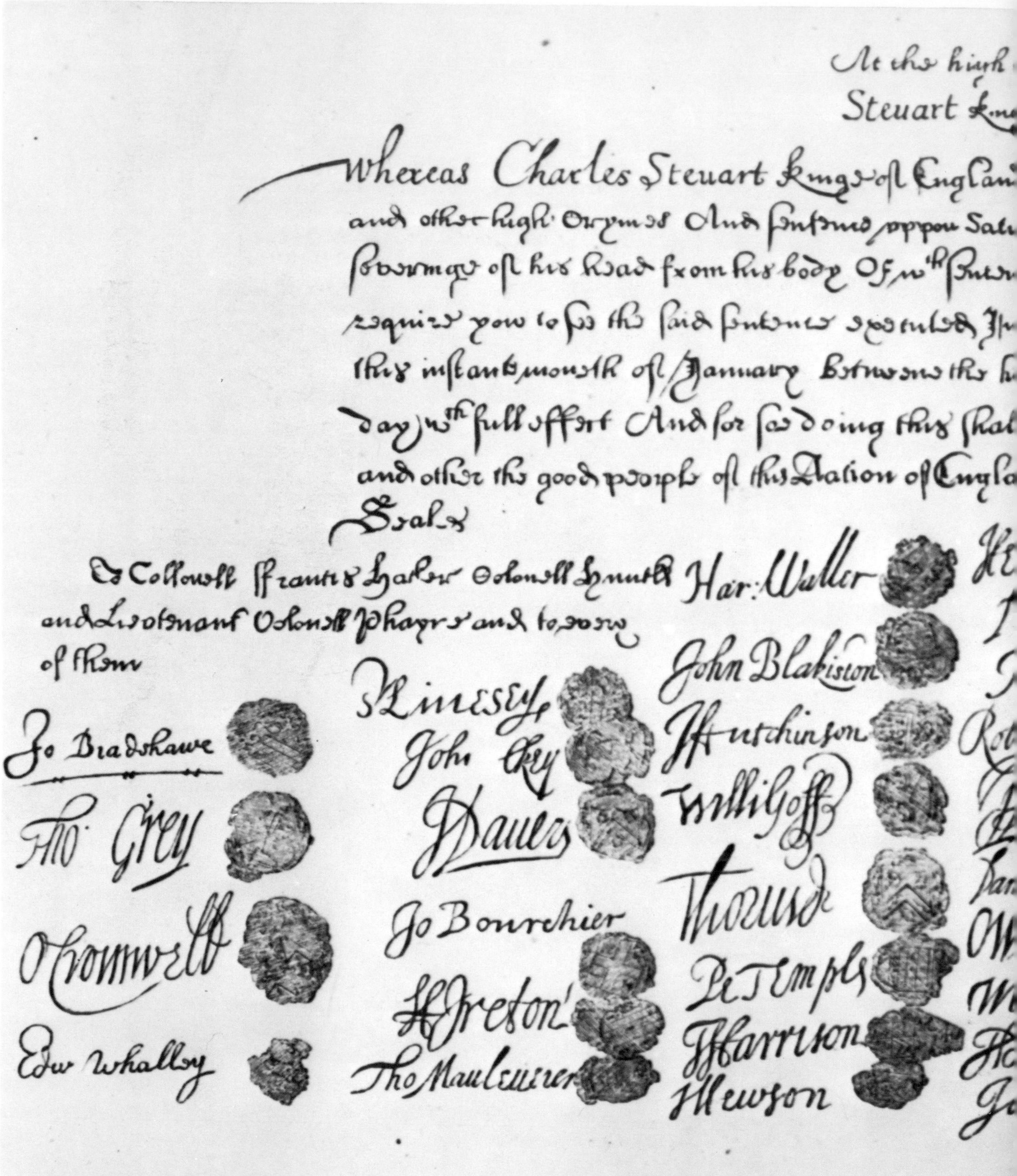
At the high
Steuart King

Whereas Charles Steuart Kinge of England
and other high Crymes And sentence uppon Satur
severinge of his head from his body Of wch sentence
require you to see the said sentence executed In the
this instant month of January Betweene the h
day wth full effect And for so doing this shal
and other the good people of this Nation of Engla
Seale

To Collonell ffrancis Hacker Collonell Huncks and Leiutenant Collonell Phayre and to every of them

Jo Bradshawe
Tho Grey
O Cromwell
Edw Whalley
M Livesey
John Okey
J Danvers
Jo Bourchier
H Ireton
Tho Mauleverer
Har: Waller
John Blakiston
J Hutchinson
Willi Goffe
Tho Pride
Pe Temple
T Harrison
J Hewson

...ffirs for the tryinge and indginge of Charles

...ngland January xxixth Anno Dm 1648.

...standeth conbicted attaynted and condemned of high treason
...war
...aft: pronounced against him by this Cort to be putt to death by the
...ion yet remayneth to be done. Thes are therfore to will and — —
...Streets before Whitehall uppon the morrow being the Thirtieth .. day of
...tenn in the morninge and ffive in the afternoone of the same —
...ffirient warrant And thes are to require All Officers and Souldiers
...assistinge unto you in this service Given under o' hands and

Jo Barkstead

King Charles I from a miniature illuminated on Letters Patent. The King wears the Order of the Garter and carries the Orb and Sceptre with the Dove.

An early photograph of Queen Victoria, aged about thirty-five, with her husband Prince Albert of Saxe-Coburg-Gotha, taken in 1854.

delegate her duties to the Prince of Wales, if she were not prepared to undertake them herself.

The situation was saved by Disraeli, who became Prime Minister in 1874. He saw in the Throne the symbol of continuity and stability and so championed the idea of monarchy at the same time using his considerable charm to encourage the Queen to resume her ceremonial functions. His blandishments, combined with the ever increasing prosperity and power of the nation, carried the day to such an extent that Victoria's reign ended in a blaze of glory and triumphalism unparalleled since the days of Good Queen Bess.

From all this, one lesson must be learned and one conclusion drawn, namely that the continuance of the Victorian or Albertian style of monarchy depends to a great extent on the personality and behaviour of the monarch and, to a lesser extent, on that of the immediate and involved Royal Family. This was forcibly underlined in 1936 when Edward VIII came to the throne. As Prince of Wales he enjoyed a popularity bordering on adulation. Everyone thought that his reign would be happier and more glorious than any in living memory. Yet, within a year, his wish to marry a divorced American lady had precipitated a crisis which, if it had not been dealt with swiftly and in a dignified way, could have spelled the end of the monarchy. Tolerance can turn to intolerance overnight and therein lies danger.

Chapter 4

The Coronation

The greatest and most important and significant ceremony of state is the coronation of a sovereign, but even the word 'coronation' is deceptive as it suggests that the whole ceremony centres on the crowning, whereas this is but one of the elements of the ceremony and by no means the most important.

In primitive societies kings were raised up and set upon stones or ceremonial seats above their people to symbolize their superiority and they were also invested with symbolic regalia. The ancient Egyptian kings bore the shepherd's crook and the cornflail to indicate that they led their people and saw to it that they were fed. Archaeological excavations have revealed ceremonial insignia such as maces and swords, which were incidents of the jurisdiction of tribal chiefs who lived as long before the birth of Christ as we live after it. The foundations of the ceremony of making a king go back to times long before recorded history.

It is not really surprising that so many Christian festivals and traditions have absorbed earlier pagan rituals; it is just part of the evolution of forms of human behaviour. So, when Christianity was re-introduced into England, or more truly into Kent, by St Augustine in the early seventh century, and during that century spread throughout the country, the concept of Christian kingship was grafted onto the not incompatible heathen idea of kingship. The pagan king – a mixture of high priest, magician and demi-god, being law-giver, protector and provider – was easily succeeded by the Christian king, enjoying the same privileges and responsibilities, but receiving all his powers and prerogatives from the triune Christian God through His established, infallible, visible Church on earth. The manner of making a king of England was first set down when St Dunstan, Archbishop of Canterbury, crowned King Edgar at Bath in 973, although earlier kings had been crowned

at Kingston-upon-Thames. This 'Edgar Ordo' or service has formed the basis of the coronation service used for nearly a thousand years. It combines the ancient pagan ceremonies of enthroning and investiture with the Christian Frankish ceremony of anointing and sacring and includes the king's contract with his subjects in the form of the king's oath and the vassal's homage. All this was enshrined within the kernel of Christian worship, the Mass. It thus established the essentially Christian character of kingship and the right – indeed the necessity – of the Church, in the person of the Archbishop of Canterbury, to perform the ceremonies.

As earlier kings had been crowned at Kingston-upon-Thames, so named because there rested the king's stone or coronation seat, so also were Edgar's successors until St Edward the Confessor's coronation which took place at Winchester in 1043. St Edward built the Abbey of St Peter at Westminster, as legend has it, at the command of St Peter himself. He built it as a church for future coronations, with a wide area, or theatre as it is called, between the transepts.

Here, in Edward's great Abbey, King Harold was crowned and after him William the Conqueror and every other sovereign of England save for Edward V and Edward VIII who, in a sense, were sovereigns-designate as they were never anointed, or crowned.

As the coronation is a Christian, sacramental ceremony, the anointing with holy oil is the outward sign of the inward grace given by God to a Christian sovereign. The placing of a crown upon the head of the Lord's anointed is the most dramatic gesture of the ceremony, and the crown itself is the popular symbol of sovereignty. This is why the monarch, whether a king or a queen, is referred to in a constitutional context as 'the Crown'.

St Dunstan's Coronation Ordo was revised and

extended slightly by Archbishop Anselm, the somewhat unwilling defender of the rights of the Church during the reigns of William II and Henry I. A further revision was made by Abbot Litlyngton and was embodied in his splendid illuminated missal, which is still preserved in the library of Westminster Abbey and which is known as the *Liber Regalis*.

This new recension of the coronation ceremony and service was probably first used in July 1377 when the boy king, Richard II, was crowned a few weeks after his grandfather's death. Thereafter it became the standard ceremonial. King James I had it translated into English for his coronation in 1603 and for the coronation of James II in 1685 it had to be greatly emasculated as James and his queen, being Roman Catholics, could not receive communion at the hands of the anglican Archbishop Sancroft. In fact, they attended a special Mass held at Whitehall on the eve of the coronation.

The coronation of King Harold in 1066. This is generally thought to have taken place at Westminster Abbey.

The Communion Service was restored at the coronation of the joint sovereigns, William III and Mary II in 1689. There also had to be a slight remodelling of the ceremony to cope with a double coronation, but the most significant alteration was that made by Dr Henry Compton, Bishop of London, who was officiating at this coronation, Archbishop Sandford having excused himself as he, like many others, was unhappy with the precipitous way in which William and Mary had been invited to occupy the throne. The new oath precluded any possibility of a Roman Catholic sovereign ever again sitting on the throne. Henceforth the sovereign swore to maintain the Protestant Reformed Religion established by law and to maintain and preserve inviolably the settlement of the Church of England and the doctrine, discipline and government thereof, as by law established in England.

During the eighteenth century the anointing and

religious part of the coronation became more and more a formality, culminating in the fantastic coronation of King George IV in 1821. The King obtained a grant of £243,000 from Parliament to enable him to stage an extravagant pageant. Those taking part were put into 'romantick' clothes with ruffs and knee breeches. Westminster Abbey was draped with scarlet cloth and Westminster Hall, from which the King proceeded to the Abbey and to which he returned after the ceremony for the banquet had been totally transformed. A wooden floor had been laid with tiers of galleries for the spectators. A vast table, at which the peers would eat, seated in gothic chairs, ran the length of the hall, at the north end of which was a triumphal gothic arch thirty feet high and thirty-six feet wide. The procession from the Hall to the Abbey seemed endless and was led, for the last time in history, by the King's Herb Woman (Mrs Fellowes) accompanied by her six maids, strewing the way with herbs. In his *Prince of Pleasure* Mr J.B. Priestley suggests that when George became King he also became more devout. 'There was an odd insistence on a simpler and more sincere piety' he writes.

This is somewhat at variance with Mrs Arbuthnot's eye witness account of the coronation as recorded in her diary. 'The King', she wrote, 'behaved very indecently; he was continually nodding and winking at Lady Conyngham and sighing and making eyes at her. At one time in the Abbey he took a diamond brooch from his breast and, looking at her, kissed it, on which she took off her glove and kissed a ring she had on!!! Anybody who could have seen his disgusting figure, with a wig the curls of which hung down his back, and quite bending beneath the weight of his robes and his *60* years would have been quite sick . . .'.

This vulgar display of worldly pomp and grandeur may have amused those who saw it, but it did not commend itself to those who had to pay for it, at a time when the poor were suffering from the miseries of the Industrial Revolution and were clamouring for reform of the franchise and for freedom of religion. It was very nearly the last coronation.

When William IV succeeded his brother in 1830 he made it clear that he did not want a coronation. 'This is my coronation' he is said to have remarked when he opened his first Parliament. He was acutely aware of the need for economy, the 'burlesque bustling old fellow' was not deeply religious and doubtless saw no spiritual significance in the ceremony and, in any case, he disliked dressing up and was happiest in old clothes among his large family of bastards, all siblings of Mrs Dorothy Jordan, 'Little Pickle', who had died fourteen years before he came to the throne. But it was

not to be. He was persuaded to go through with the ceremony, but the cost was cut so drastically that William's coronation has been aptly described as a 'half-crownation'.

The principal saving was effected by abandoning the procession from Westminster Hall and the banquet held there after the ceremony. This meant that the Hall was not used at all and so did not have to be decorated. These parts of the pageantry surrounding a coronation have now gone forever, although I believe it would be popular and no great extravagance if the outside procession from Buckingham Palace were to go to Westminster Hall, rather than the Abbey. The inside procession could then form up in the Hall as of old and proceed, along a raised platform to the Abbey, thus enabling many thousands of people to see the great panoply and magnificence of the Great Procession. After the ceremony, the procession could return to the Hall by the same route.

The religious character of the ceremony was restored when Queen Victoria was crowned, although an article in *The Times* stated 'the anointing is a part of the ceremony more recommended by antiquity than delicacy, and will probably be omitted altogether'. Such was not the case, the young Queen was deeply moved by the symbolic and historic nature of the coronation ceremony and would not have any part of it left out. That she did not dwell on the sacramental nature of the ceremony in her diary is perhaps not surprising, when the whole day must have been so moving and emotional for a girl who had just celebrated her nineteenth birthday, but her account of coronation day leaves one in no doubt as to the deep significance which she attached to the ceremony. At the same time, there are hints in her account of her sense of humour, sentimentality, intolerance and partiality, as when she writes:

> Poor old Lord Rolle who is 82, and dreadfully infirm, in attempting to ascend the steps fell and rolled quite down (at the homage) . . . When my good Lord Melbourne knelt down and kissed my hand, he pressed my hand and I grasped his with all my heart . . . I then repaired . . . to St Edward's Chapel, as it is called; but which, as Lord Melbourne said, was more *un*like a Chapel than anything he had ever seen; for what was *called* an *Altar* was covered with sandwiches, bottles of wine, etc., etc. The Archbishop came in and *ought* to have delivered the orb to me, but I had already got it, and he (as usual) was *so* confused and puzzled and knew nothing and – went away.

Then the whole account is permeated with her affection for her 'kind impartial friend . . . my excellent Lord Melbourne . . . my kind Lord Melbourne.'

Let us now look closely at the actual coronation ceremony and service and in doing so learn something of the symbols and the symbolism.

Originally, there were thirteen principal elements in the great ceremony. The first four and the last did not survive King George IV's coronation, namely the occupation of the Tower of London by the claimant to the throne on the eve of the coronation (this in fact was abandoned by James II); his progress through the cities of London and Westminster to Westminster Hall the next morning (for this the progress from Buckingham Palace to the Abbey and back may be regarded as a substitute); the enthronement in Westminster Hall; the procession from the Hall to the Abbey and the banquet after the service.

Richard II was the first king to spend the eve of his coronation in the Tower. This was done to show that he was master of the very independent City of London. The procession the next day was to show the sovereign-elect to the people. In Westminster Hall the king was raised up 'with all gentleness and reverence' and placed upon the King's Bench or seat of justice. The Court of the King's Bench (at present, of course, called Queen's Bench) was essentially the Common Law court over which the king especially, and until the time of King Henry IV, actually, presided. It was the last court of law to break away from the Council. It was here that the king was recognized by his peers and in the *Liber Regalis* it is called the 'election' which would later be confirmed by a representative selection of the people in the Abbey. After the election, the solemn religious procession was formed together with the royal procession with the regalia bearers and this great and colourful company moved to the Abbey.

The banquet after the ceremony provided an opportunity for various serjeantries to be performed. Serjeantry is best described as a feudal service rendered to the Sovereign by a subject in respect of tenure of lands or tenements. For example, the Lord of the Manor of Liston in Essex holds his manor by virtue of making and serving wafers at a coronation. He is, therefore, called the King's Waferer and claims for his fee all the instruments of silver and other metal used in this service, with the linen and liveries for himself and two men. The last to perform this office was Mr John Campbell of Liston in 1821.

The Lord of the Manor of Bardolf, or Addington presented a 'mess of dillegrout' or 'malpigeryun' at the banquet. At George IV's banquet the Archbishop of Canterbury held the manor of Addington by virtue of this serjeantry and so performed the service by

King George IV being crowned at Westminster Abbey on 10 July 1821.

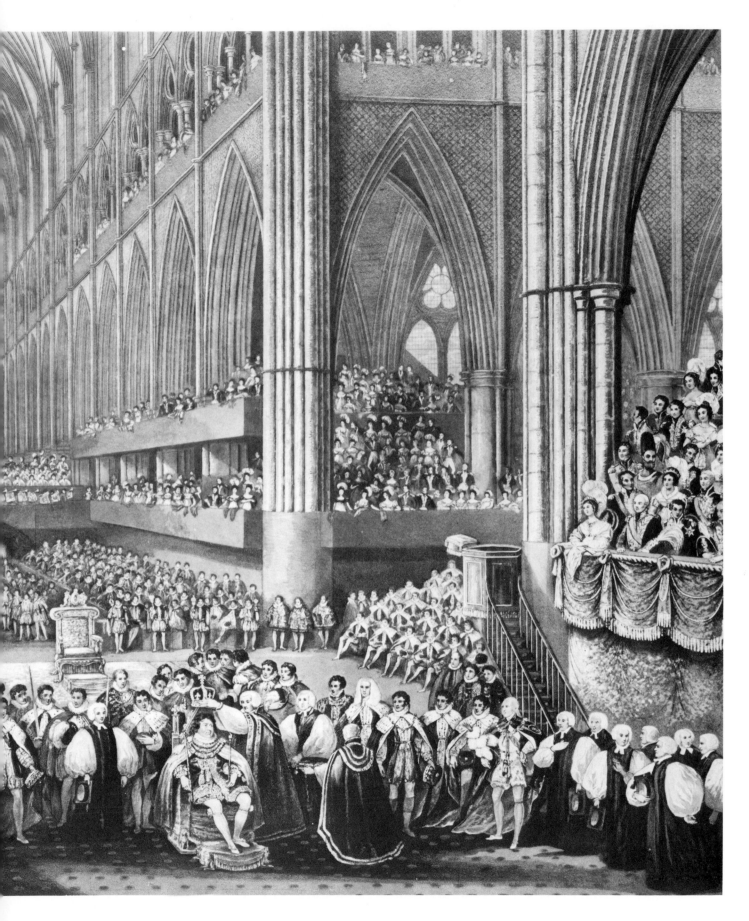

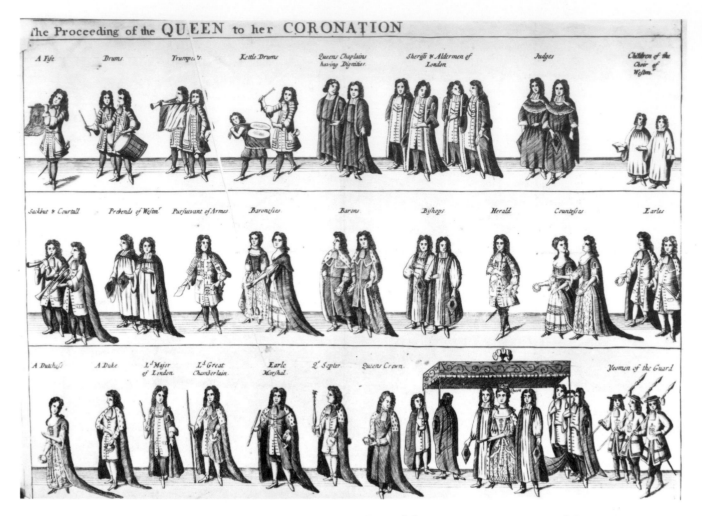

Part of the coronation procession of Queen Anne in 1702.

deputy. The Manor of Great Wymondley was held by the serjeantry of serving the king and queen with the first silver-gilt cup, which the Lord of the Manor kept as his fee. These and many more serjeantries are now historic and unlikely to be revived.

Those parts of the full Ceremonial which are still observed will become apparent in the pages which follow. For convenience, as well as interest, I have used as a point of departure the coronation of Her present Majesty, in the arrangements of which I was privileged to play a very minor role as a member of the Earl Marshal's ceremonial staff.

Coronations used to follow fairly swiftly upon the succession of a sovereign. This was partly for practical reasons, because until he had been anointed a mediaeval king must have felt a trifle insecure and partly because the ceremony did not take so long to prepare as a modern coronation, where the whole Commonwealth has to be considered and consulted, not to mention the moguls of the media. Henry III was crowned on the ninth day after John's decease, and

Edward III on the eleventh day after his father's death. As time went on, the interval between accession and coronation tended to increase but the fifty-three weeks delay before Queen Victoria's coronation was sufficiently unusual to cause the following comment in the *Law Times* of 16 February 1901: 'the delay was probably due to the need of ascertaining with certainty that no issue would be born of the King's Consort. And, moreover, it is reported, with some aspect of credibility, that Her Majesty was so slight as to be at an earlier date unable to bear, for the necessarily long period the coronation involves, the weight of the Regalia'. The reference to the 'King's Consort' is to the widow of William IV, Queen Adelaide, who was almost, but probably not quite, past child-bearing in 1837.

The 1953 coronation took a year to prepare. This was for the reasons I have mentioned and also because, with such enormous exposure and press interest throughout the world, it had to be done not just well but supremely well.

No, the politicians may have shown less imagination than we had, perhaps over-optimistically, expected but Sir George Bellew, Garter King of Arms, and so the Earl Marshal's principal aide-de-camp, was a man unusually endowed with historical sensitivity, artistic ability and imagination. Under the guidance and leadership of Sir George Bellew, Garter King of Arms, all that could be done to make the occasion magnificent and memorable was done. His flair, coupled with the Earl Marshal's (the late Bernard, Duke of Norfolk) command of ceremony made Her Majesty's coronation one of the greatest in our history.

I and others working for the Earl Marshal and Sir George, spent several months before the coronation was officially proclaimed, going through histories and ceremonials of coronations, so that any decisions that might later have to be made would be made with the full knowledge and understanding of ancient precedents.

The official starting gun was fired on 6 June 1952 when, by an Order in Council, the Earl Marshal was commanded to have the coronation proclaimed at the usual times and places and with the usual solemnity. By this proclamation all those who, by reason of their offices and tenures, save those 'anciently done and performed in Westminster Hall or the Procession' to attend 'in all respects furnished and appointed as to so great a solemnity appertaineth'. If they failed so to do they were warned that they would answer 'at their perils'.

Ten days later a committee of the Privy Council appointed an executive committee to make preliminary arrangements. This committee consisted of the Archbishop of Canterbury, the Lord Chamberlain, Garter King of Arms and twenty-three other gentlemen, under the chairmanship of the Earl Marshal. It also ordered the Archbishop to 'inspect the Office of Divine Service to be used'.

A few months later the Earl Marshal set up his official coronation office at 14 Belgrave Square, which had been prepared for him by the Ministry of Works, although it was not until 28 November that he was officially charged by the Privy Council to make all the necessary arrangements.

In February 1953 the Home Secretary, Sir David Maxwell-Fyfe (later Viscount Kilmuir), was commanded to arrange for the access and regress of carriages. In March the Earl Marshal was ordered to cause 9000 copies of the Order of Service to be printed, after the Queen had approved it, and also to publish the Ceremonial and cause it 'to be punctually observed in every particular thereof'.

In turn the Earl Marshal ordered the Lord Chamberlain of the Household, the Earl of Scarborough, to furnish all the regalia, right down to an 'oblation bason', an ingot of twenty-two carat gold in a crimson velvet bag with gilt cords, and silver truncheons for the High Constables of England and Scotland.

In fact, with her Majesty's permission, various items to be employed in the ceremony were donated. For example, The Scriveners' Company of London presented the pen with which the Queen subscribed the Oath and the Girdlers' Company presented the Stole Royal. It was Sir George Bellew's suggestion that the armils or bracelets, which had not been used since James I's coronation, should be reintroduced. A pair of ornate bracelets existed, but it was decided to make a new pair to be presented by the governments of the Commonwealth Countries and of Southern Rhodesia. The armils were made by the Goldsmiths and Silversmiths Company at a cost of £520. They were of plain gold with a narrow decorative edge and a clasp in the form of a Tudor rose. They were lined with red velvet and inside was engraved: 'Presented for the Coronation of Her Majesty Queen Elizabeth II by the Governments of the United Kingdom, Canada, Australia, New Zealand, South Africa, Pakistan, Ceylon and Southern Rhodesia'.

The principal concerns of the Earl Marshal's Office were the actual Ceremonial, the seating in the Abbey and co-ordination with the ecclesiastical authorities, the Ministry of Works, Police, caterers and the Armed Services.

To deal with the media the Earl Marshal set up a Press Bureau, with Mr R.G.S. Hoare (Chief Information Officer at the Ministry of National Insurance and a former journalist) as the principal Press Officer. Under his able direction, the Earl Marshal made history by holding a Press conference: this was something no Earl Marshal had ever done before. On 3 March 1953, over 200 journalists, photographers, newsreel and television men gathered at Church House, Westminster. The Earl Marshal told them exactly what we were doing and then answered a barrage of questions. I hope that the late Earl Marshal would forgive me if I described his expression in repose as 'po-faced'. It totally belied his real character and, at first gave people the wrong impression. He had a very real, but never mordant wit and when he made one of his slightly mischievous remarks wrinkles of mirth would appear round his eyes and if ever eyes could truly be described as 'blue and twinkling', they were his. I re-read the transcript of this historic conference recently and was once again filled with admiration for the simple, courteous, able, honest and amusing way in which he replied to the

THE ROD WITH THE DOVE	SAINT EDWARD'S CROWN	THE ORB
borne by	*borne by*	*borne by*
The Duke of Richmond and Gordon	THE LORD HIGH STEWARD Admiral of the Fleet the Viscount Cunningham of Hyndhope, K.T., G.C.B., O.M., D.S.O.	Field-Marshal the Earl Alexander of Tunis, K.G., G.C.B., G.C.M.G., C.S.I., D.S.O., M.C.
his coronet carried by his page	*attended by his two pages*	*his coronet carried by his page*
Simon Benton-Jones, Esq.	Julian James, Esq., *and* Martin Brett, Esq.	Hon. Brian Alexander

THE PATEN	THE BIBLE	THE CHALICE
borne by	*borne by*	*borne by*
THE BISHOP OF LONDON	THE BISHOP OF NORWICH	THE BISHOP OF WINCHESTER
The Right Reverend William Wand, D.D.	The Right Reverend Percy M. Herbert, D.D.	The Right Reverend Alwyn T. P. Williams, D.D.

The Clerk of the Cheque and Adjutant (Lt.-Colonel Hon. Osbert Vesey, C.M.G., C.B.E.) and Ten Gentlemen-at-Arms

THE BISHOP OF BATH AND WELLS
The Right Reverend Harold William Bradfield, D.D.

THE QUEEN

In Her Royal Robe of Crimson Velvet, trimmed with Ermine and bordered with Gold Lace; wearing the Collar of the Garter; on Her Head a Diadem of Precious Stones

Her Majesty's Train borne by
THE MISTRESS OF THE ROBES
The Duchess Dowager of Devonshire
assisted by

THE BISHOP OF DURHAM
The Right Reverend Arthur Michael Ramsay, D.D.

The Lieutenant (Brigadier-General Sir Harvey Kearsley, K.C.V.O., C.M.G., D.S.O.) and Ten Gentlemen-at-Arms

Lady Jane Vane-Tempest-Stewart
Lady Anne Coke
Lady Moyra Hamilton

Lady Mary Baillie-Hamilton
Lady Jane Heathcote-Drummond-Willoughby
Lady Rosemary Spencer-Churchill

the coronet of the Mistress of the Robes carried by her page
Marquess of Hartington

THE GROOM OF THE ROBES
Captain Sir Harold Campbell, K.C.V.O., D.S.O., R.N.

LADIES OF THE BEDCHAMBER

Countess of Euston   The Countess of Leicester

WOMEN OF THE BEDCHAMBER

Lady Alice Egerton   Lady Margaret Hay
Mrs. Alexander Abel Smith   Hon. Mrs. Andrew Elphinstone

25

plethora of questions both on matters of principle and detail. It was quite obvious from the tone of the questions, as the conference continued, that he was winning the Press over to his side by sheer force of character, in fact, by being himself. So successful was this conference that another was held on the 12 May which was attended by almost twice the number of those present in March. His victory of the Press was total after he had given two cocktail parties for leading British and Commonwealth journalists at his home in Chester Street.

Our first main and continuing concern was to plot all the movements in the actual ceremony. To this end we had printed plans of the theatre on which every single move was plotted. In addition, we had a huge master plan of the Abbey and pins inscribed on the top with the name of everyone taking part in the ceremony. Different coloured pins were used to denote the various categories of participant. We used to play with these pins and then, when we had worked out a movement which seemed proper and dignified, we would transpose this onto one of our printed plans and then try the next movement. It was all great fun but, in retrospect, perhaps almost too elaborate.

While this was going on, we were drafting the actual Ceremonial. Here we often needed to consult the Queen to make sure that what we were planning met with her approval and we used to make out a list of questions for the Earl Marshal to put to her. Like the Earl Marshal, the Queen was always ready to give quick and unequivocal answers. Looking at one of these questionnaires recently, I was not really surprised to find that the answers to almost all the questions were monosyllabic and all were definitive. The longest answer was 'Refer to P.C.' – that is to the Privy Council.

One thing the Queen had to do fairly early on in the proceedings was to appoint certain officers and regalia bearers as these had to be included in the Ceremonial. This she did and the Court of Claims had to sit in order to judge various people's claims to be present, or to perform services as of right.

The Court of Claims seems first to have sat before the coronation of Richard II in 1377, under the presidency of the Steward of the Household, later called the Lord High Steward. Today, it is a Commission of the Privy Council and it is empowered to hear and determine all claims except those services previously performed at the banquet.

The court which sat before the Queen's coronation allowed the following claims: the Dean and Chapter

Opposite: *A page from the official Ceremonial of the coronation of Queen Elizabeth II.*

of Westminster to assist the Archbishop of Canterbury; the Bishops of Durham and Bath and Wells to support the Queen throughout the ceremony; the Barons of the Cinque Ports to carry a canopy; the Walker Trustees by virtue of holding the office of Hereditary Usher of the White Rod and Principal Usher of Scotland, to be present by deputy but not to perform any duties; Lyon King of Arms and the Scottish Officers of Arms to be present but not to perform any duties; the Clerk of the Crown to record the proceedings but his claim to be furnished with five yards of scarlet cloth to be referred to Her Majesty; the Countess of Erroll as High Constable of Scotland to be present by deputy approved by the Queen and to be provided with a baton; the Earl of Shrewsbury, if invited as Lord High Steward of Ireland, to carry a white wand; the Lord Great Chamberlain, the Marquess of Cholmondeley, to execute his duties and services; the Lord Mayor of London, if it were the Queen's pleasure, to attend and bear the crystal mace; Lords Hastings and Churston to carry the golden spurs and the Viscount Dudhope (whose claim to the Earldom of Dundee was allowed before the coronation) to carry the Royal Standard of Scotland as Hereditary Royal Standard Bearer of Scotland.

No order was made on claims to carry a towel, find three maple cups and bear the Queen's cup, as these were services connected with the banquet.

The claim of The Fort George Land Company Limited, as owners of the Manor of Worksop, to provide a glove – an ancient service of that manor – was disallowed after argument. It was held that a Limited Company could not perform a feudal service. Likewise the Duke of Somerset's claim to carry the Orb or the Sceptre with the Cross or to perform such other services as the Queen might determine, was not admitted as it was found that although previous dukes had sometimes performed services at coronations, this was not of right, but by the grace of the Sovereign. Finally, no order was made on a quite ludicrous claim to attend by a man calling himself His Highness the Prince O'Brien of Thomond.

One of the Earl Marshal's early duties was to issue dress regulations. Because of the cost of new peers' and peeresses' robes and coronets, Mr (the late Sir) Norman Hartnell was invited to design a modified form of peeresses' robe. The robes of state of a peeress consisted of a kirtle of crimson velvet with a narrow edging of miniver pure, gathered at the back in three festoons, each tied with a bow of golden tinsel. The sleeves were to be about nine inches long, each sleeve having two bands of miniver pure around it. Over this was worn a mantle of crimson velvet with a train, the whole edged with and having a cape of miniver pure

49

with rows or bars of ermine tails. The length of the train varied from three feet for a baroness to six feet for a duchess and the number of rows of ermine tails on the cape also varied according to the rank of the wearer. A baroness had two and a duchess four rows. The whole outfit together with an appropriate coronet of silver-gilt with its cap of velvet turned up with ermine, fashioned in the best materials, cost about £475, which was a lot of money in 1952.

Eventually, Mr Hartnell came up with a design which the Earl Marshal liked and of which the Queen signified her approval, but only baronesses and viscountesses were permitted to wear it. Presumably countesses and above were expected to be able to afford the real thing. In the Earl Marshal's Regulations issued in December 1952 the alternative robe is described thus: 'A Robe of Crimson velvet, trimmed with miniver pure, two inches in width similar in style to a Kirtle, but without sleeves and with the addition of a cape also of miniver pure and shaped like a cape collar, finishing in two points in front of the waist. The cape is to have rows or bars of ermine tails (or the like) as follows:

A BARONESS: two rows of ermine tails
A VISCOUNTESS: two rows and a half of ermine tails.

It was a sort of amalgam of robe and kirtle and could be made for £10. 15s. 6d (£10.75p). Obviously, this involved a little cheating. Miniver or Minever really only means *menu vair* or small fur. It was the fur of small animals often but not exclusively that of the ermine in its winter coat, so perhaps it is permissible to construe it as embracing coney, but its interpretation was also further extended in 1952 to cover a man-made fabric called Ermaleen. Because of the cost of silver-gilt coronets, a cap, not unlike that worn

inside a coronet, was designed for baronesses and viscountesses. These caps cost a mere £1. 5s. 8d (£1.27p), but I honestly cannot recollect seeing many on Coronation Day.

The Earl Marshal's orders regarding coronets specifies that they shall be made of silver-gilt and that no jewels or precious stones may adorn them, nor counterfeit pearls be used in place of the silver balls which, in varying numbers and sizes, are to be found on the coronets of barons, viscounts, earls and marquesses and of their wives whose coronets are of the same design, but smaller. The circlets of coronets of all degrees, except the degree of baron and baroness are to be chased or engraved with representations of jewels. This order was the subject of a humorous verse by 'The Fool of Arms' (that is Mr C.W. Scott-Giles) in his *Motley Heraldry*.

Lord Bumptious and Lord Gumptious, with the coronation near,
Went out to get their coronets, like many a noble peer.
Lord Bumptious went to Bond Street in a costly limousine
And interviewed a goldsmith (by appointment to the Queen)
And he was most particular, and made a lot of fuss.
Lord Gumptious made for Wardour Street. He went there on a bus.
Lord Bumptious placed an order for a rim of finest gold
Encrusted with as many precious stones as it would hold,
And thereon six enormous balls of iridescent nacre.
Lord Gumptious sought the office of a certain stage-prop maker
And hired a gilded circlet set with silvered balls – quite tinny
But correct in every detail, and it cost him half-a-guinea.
At the Abbey the Earl Marshal said, 'Lord Bumptious, stand aside.
To deck a coronet with gems to every peer's denied.
A baron can't have beaded baubles winking at the brim
When e'en a Duke thinks 'chased as jewelled' good enough for him.
And where you should have silver balls you've got those lustrous spheres
Like the illuminations that you find on seaside piers
You can't come in, my noble Lord – your coronet's too swell . . .
Your coronet, Lord Gumptious? Thank you. Pass, my Lord – all's well.

The coronet of a Peer is to be of silver gilt, the cap of crimson velvet turned up with ermine, with a golden tassel on the top, the circlet having on its rim, in the case of:

A BARON: Six silver balls on the rim of equal size and at equal distances.

A VISCOUNT: Sixteen silver balls on the rim, all of equal size.

AN EARL: Eight silver balls, raised on points, with golden strawberry leaves between the points, very slightly raised.

A MARQUESS: Four golden strawberry leaves and four silver balls alternately, all very slightly raised and all of equal height.

A DUKE: Eight golden strawberry leaves, very slightly raised, and all of equal height.

No jewels or precious stones may adorn the coronets of Peers, nor counterfeit pearls be used instead of silver balls. The circlets of coronets

Details of peers' coronets from the Earl Marshal's dress regulations for the Queen's coronation.

Peers in robes and wearing their coronets leaving Westminster Abbey after the coronation of George V in 1911.

I have quoted this not only for light relief, but also because it contains an element of truth, in that there actually was a flourishing business in hiring out very tinny theatrical coronets before the coronation.

No dress concessions were made for peers. They had to produce a robe which at least looked like a robe 'of crimson velvet, edged down the front with miniver pure, with rows or bars of ermine tails (or the like) according to degree'.

Ladies were to wear evening or afternoon dresses with 'light veiling falling from the back of the head'. Gentlemen could wear the robes of Orders of Knighthood if appropriate, ceremonial or full dress if in the services, full dress or levee dress if in the Civil, Foreign or Colonial Service or one of the forms of Court Dress as laid down in the Lord Chamberlain's Regulations for dress at court. Even with a modified Court Dress it was obvious that many could not afford to hire it, let alone buy it, so gentlemen were also permitted to wear evening dress with either knee breeches or trousers, morning dress, or *faute de mieux* dark lounge suits. This was right, but it was a pity that it was.

The seating department of the Earl Marshal's office was master-minded by Mr (later Sir) John Heaton-

Armstrong, Chester Herald. Assisted by other heralds and a bevy of beautiful girls he had to see that everyone attending was given the right seat and all the necessary instructions with regard to dress, parking and so forth. It was a truly democratic, if I may misuse that much abused word, coronation in that representatives from all walks of life were invited to be present. The Earl Marshal and his advisers had to work out a comprehensive list for the Queen's approval and then hand it over to the seating department for action. To make more room for a wider cross-section of people than at previous coronations the number of seats available for peers and their wives was restricted and a ballot held. This and the provision by the Ministry of Works of as many seats as it was humanly and safely possible to squeeze into the Abbey, certainly eased the situation. In the end everyone saw something but in many cases it was very little.

Our own interest in the seating was simply the provision of an invitation card. We invited selected artists to submit designs and in the end the Queen approved an elegant design, incorporating floral emblems of Commonwealth Countries, submitted by Miss Joan Hassall. We had prints taken in a variety of colours, but in the end blue was chosen. Indeed, blue and gold were the colours which characterized the coronation, for both the carpets in the Abbey and the coverings of the chairs and stools were in these colours.

The only other office at Belgrave Square was the Gold Staff Officers' department. Gold Staff Officers are the ushers at a coronation, so called because, as a symbol of their office and authority, they carry gilded staves. They are appointed by the Earl Marshal, acting on behalf of the Queen. There were about 300 such officers and they were commanded by Major General Randle (later Sir Randle) Feilden. They should not be confused with Gold-Stick, who is more properly called Gold-Stick-in-Waiting, and is the Colonel (usually a retired officer) of one of the two regiments of the Household Cavalry, the Life Guards and the Blues and Royals.

The seating in the Abbey was divided into blocks of seats in various areas, such as the transcepts, nave, triforium and so forth. Each block was placed under the care of a Gold Staff Officer, who was strictly confined to the area under his command. It was his duty to see to the needs of those seated in his block and to control their departure after the ceremony. There were other officers, like myself, who had specific duties. Mine were to conduct the Lord High Steward's pages to the South Transept after the procession had entered; then, after the crowning, Mr John Cordle,

The invitation to attend the Queen's coronation, designed by Miss Joan Hassall.

sometime Member of Parliament for Bournemouth East and Christchurch, and I, brought in the faldstools (really *prie-dieux*) and placed them before the altar for the Queen and the Duke of Edinburgh's communion. After the service I and other special Gold Staff Officers (we were distinguished by having two strips of yellow ribbon on our brassards) took the regalia in procession to the Jerusalem Chamber for safe keeping before being returned to the Tower of London.

Naturally, various rehearsals had to be held and these took place during May, the final full rehearsal, which an invited audience attended, being held on 29 May. Although the Queen attended a rehearsal, the Duchess of Norfolk usually stood in for her. One of those present at the final rehearsal was Mr Tom Driberg (later Lord Bradwell) who commented that the Queen's Maids of Honour needed suntan make-up as they were too pale, that the Lord Privy Seal, Mr Harry (later Viscount) Crookshank stood with his legs apart, that the Archbishop of Canterbury needed to practise singing the Preface and that the Knights of the Garter who held the canopy over the Queen were jerky, which is not really surprising, considering that one of them suffered from Parkinson's disease. However, on the great day itself all went perfectly.

For the Gold Staff Officers the day began at 5.30 a.m. and an excellent breakfast was provided in a vast marquee in Dean's Yard. The guests too had to arrive early as the Abbey doors were closed to them at 8.30. At 8.50 the minor members of the Royal Family were

Opposite: *The Lord Chancellor handing the Queen the Gracious Speech at the State Opening of Parliament in 1979.*

conducted, in procession, to their places by two Pursuivants. In fact, Officers of Arms led all the processions of various dignitaries. After the 'minor royals' came the royal and other representatives of foreign states. Almost every country in the world was represented, even down to the tiny Republic of San Marino (population then about 13,000). They walked strictly in order of diplomatic precedence. After the foreign representatives came the rulers of states under the Queen's protection. Among these were such colourful characters as the Tungku Ampuan of Selangor and Queen Salote of Tonga, whose splendid presence and total disregard of the rain, which sadly characterized Coronation Day, almost stole the show during the outside procession.

The next procession walked not towards, but from the High Altar. It consisted of the Dean and Prebendaries of Westminster, bearing the regalia, preceded by the choir singing the litany. They placed the regalia on a richly furbished table in the Annexe; this was the extension built outside the West Door of the Abbey for the occasion. I have never discovered why it was spelled archaically, it was certainly a very up-to-date and well appointed building.

At 10.14 the Princess and Princesses of the Blood Royal arrived and were conducted to their places. It is curious that the usual rule of processing, that is *juniores priores* (juniors leading) was reversed in this procession, although not in that of Queen Elizabeth the Queen Mother and Princess Margaret, which followed hard on its heels.

At 10.38 the regalia was solemnly delivered to the peers, specially appointed by the Queen to bear the same, by the Lord Great Chamberlain, he having received the various objects from the Earl Marshal, representing the Lord High Constable, to whom they were handed by the Comptroller of the Lord Chamberlain's Office.

The Earl of Ancaster received St Edward's Staff. This is a golden rod, four feet seven inches long, tipped with steel and surmounted by an orb. It was made in 1661, the original staff having been broken up along with most of the rest of the regalia, by order of the Cromwellian Parliament. It used to be handed to the sovereign to guide him to the altar, but since the coronation of Charles II, it has been carried before him. I think it was rather a pity that we did not take the opportunity of reverting to the old rubric.

Viscount Portal of Hungerford was handed the Sceptre with the Cross, symbol of royal power and justice. It was made in 1661 but was greatly embellis-

Opposite: The Prince of Wales doing homage for the Principality at his investiture at Caernarvon Castle in 1969.

hed in 1911 when the largest portion of the famous Cullinan diamond, or Star of Africa, was inserted beneath the orb at the top in such a way that it can be removed and used separately. A little later the other sceptre, the Rod with the Dove, symbolizing equity and mercy, also made in 1661, was delivered to the Duke of Richmond and Gordon.

Before this the spurs and four swords were handed over. Lord Hastings and Lord Churston, by hereditary right allowed by the Court of Claims, each received a spur, symbol of knightly chivalry and so sometimes called St George's Spurs. The pointed Sword of Justice to the Temporality, or Third Sword, was given to the Duke of Buccleuch and Queensberry and the like Sword of Justice to the Spirituality, or Second Sword, was held by the Earl of Home (now Lord Home of the Hirschel). As 'earthly power doth... show likest God's when mercy seasons justice', the next sword presented is the Sword of Mercy, called Curtana (from the Latin *curtare*, to shorten) because, as a symbol of mercy, the point is cut off. This sword was carried by the Duke of Northumberland, and the Marquess of Salisbury bore the Sword of State.

Earl Alexander of Tunis received the Orb or Mound, which is a golden sphere ensigned by a cross, symbolizing that earthly sovereignty must be held under the Cross of Christ. Charles Greville noted in his diary that when Queen Victoria received the Orb she said to Lord John Thynne: "What am I to do with it?" "Your Majesty is to carry it, if you please, in your hand." "Am I?", she said: "it is very heavy". Perhaps she had a point, as many ritualists believe that the use of both the Orb and Sceptre with the Cross is unnecessary, in that both have the same significance.

The last and most important piece of temporal regalia to be presented was St Edward's Crown, which was carried by the Lord High Steward, Viscount Cunningham of Hyndhope. This crown, the ultimate symbol of sovereignty was made, like most of the regalia, by Sir Robert Vyner, goldsmith to Charles II in 1661. It consists of a golden rim set about with four fleurs-de-lis alternating with as many crosses formy from which rise two arches, symbolizing independent sovereignty, but surmounting them at the point of intersection is an orb and cross, once again a reminder that Christian sovereignty is exercised under the Cross. The whole crown is richly ornamented with pearls and precious stones.

After the crown had been delivered the Bishops of London, Winchester and Norwich were handed the paten, chalice and bible respectively.

Once the regalia had been delivered the Great Procession formed up in the Annexe. At eleven o'clock the royal party arrived and the Queen and the

Duke of Edinburgh went to their retiring rooms, preparatory to joining the procession, which moved off a quarter of an hour later as the choir sang the anthem 'I was glad when they said unto me, We will go into the House of the Lord'.

First came the clergy, royal chaplains, domestic chaplains, representatives of the Free Churches and Church of Scotland and the Dean and Prebendaries of Westminster. They were followed by officers of the various Orders of Knighthood. After these walked the bearers of the Standards, which were actually banners, but for some reason are invariably incorrectly described, even in official ceremonials. I should perhaps explain that a standard is a long, tapering flag, emblazoned with arms, motto, badge and crest. A banner is a rectangular flag emblazoned throughout with a coat of arms, like the one which flies over Buckingham Palace when the Queen is in residence, but which is also wrongly described as the Royal Standard.

The flags of the Commonwealth Countries were carried by their High Commissioners in London. The Union Jack, as it is commonly styled, was borne by Captain John L.M. Dymoke, the Queen's Champion.

Until the coronation banquet was discontinued the Champion performed his duty on that occasion. He rode in full armour into Westminster Hall, flanked by two gentlemen representing the Dukes of Acquitaine and Normandy. A herald then proclaimed: 'If any person . . . shall deny or gainsay, Our Sovereign Lord . . . to be Heir to the Imperial Crown of this Realm of England . . . Here is his Champion, who saith that he Lyeth, and is a False Traytor, being ready in Person to Combat with him; and in this Quarel will adventure his Life against him . . .'. The Champion then threw down the gauntlet. If no one picked it up the herald retrieved it and handed it back to the Champion. This challenge was repeated three times after which the sovereign drank to the Champion in a gilt bowl with a cover. The Champion responded and took the bowl and cover as his fee.

As the Champion has been unable to perform his office since 1821, although I can see no reason why he should not do it outside the Abbey after the ceremony and before the return to Buckingham Palace, the sovereign has graciously allowed him to carry the Union Flag. The Queen continued this custom in 1953.

The banners of Wales, the quarterings of the Royal Arms and the Royal Banner were carried by those appointed to do so by the Queen. Banners of arms were first carried at George IV's coronation in 1821. These were the banners of the arms of England, Scotland, Ireland, Hanover, (George was King of Hanover), the Union and the Royal Arms. After the coronation the Officers of Arms brought the banners back to the College of Arms, where they hung until 1902, no flags having been carried in 1831 or 1838. This acquisition of the banners was claimed as a prerogative of the Officers of Arms and from 1902 they have been brought back to the College, anyone wishing to keep the banner he carried being required to furnish the College with a replica of it. In 1953 the cost of a replica was as much as £120, the banners having been beautifully appliquèd on silk by the Royal School of Needlework.

After the banners came the Vice-Chamberlain, Treasurer and Comptroller of the Household. These offices, dubbed 'ornamental sinecures' by Mr Henry Labouchere, a radical Member of Parliament in Liberal Governments from 1865 to 1906 are purely political appointments. Mr Labouchere provided Queen Victoria with an opportunity to exercise her Prerogative. She considered that his predeliction for commenting on the Royal Family in his periodical *Truth* was scurrilous. In the words of the historian, R.C.K. Ensor, 'she laid it down to Gladstone that, though he need not exclude Labouchere from all preferment, he must not bestow on him any which would render the Queen likely to meet him personally'.

These gentlemen were followed by the Keeper of the Jewel House bearing, on a cushion, the rings,

The King's Champion entering Westminster Hall at King George IV's coronation banquet.

Pages 56–7: The Queen in her coach on the way to Westminster Abbey for her coronation in 1953.

armils and sword for the offering. Then came the Knights of the Garter appointed to carry the canopy, the Lord Privy Seal, the Prime Ministers of the Commonwealth Countries and Sir Winston Churchill wearing his robe as a Knight of the Garter, as he was then Prime Minister of the United Kingdom. Next came the Archbishop of York, the Lord High Chancellor and the Archbishop of Canterbury, preceding the Duke of Edinburgh and his entourage.

The regalia bearers followed interspersed by Kings of Arms, Great Officers of State and others. The proceeding was very much the same as at Queen Anne's coronation in 1708, for this was the only precedent for the coronation of a married, female sovereign.

Then, in the words of the official Ceremonial, came the Queen 'In her Royal Robe of Crimson Velvet, trimmed with Ermine and bordered with Gold Lace; wearing the Collar of the Garter; on Her Head a Diadem of Precious Stones'. This diadem is that made for King George IV and altered for subsequent monarchs and which, in stylized form, adorns the Queen's head on postage stamps and elsewhere.

The Queen's train was borne by the Mistress of the Robes, the Dowager Duchess of Devonshire, assisted by six Maids of Honour appointed for the occasion. They were followed by various members of the Queen's Household, with twelve Yeoman of the Guard bringing up the rear.

Upon arrival at the Theatre, or Area as it is called in the Ceremonial, all went to their places, the regalia having been laid upon the altar. The Queen, after private prayers, went to her seat and then stood for the Recognition, which is the election by the people. Attended by her trainbearers, certain Great Officers of State and preceded by Garter King of Arms, the Archbishop of Canterbury presented the Queen four times to the people – East, South, West and North, in that order, saying 'Sirs, (women's liberation was still a seed rather than a plant) I here present unto you Queen ELIZABETH, your undoubted Queen Whereof all you who are come this day to do your homage and service, Are you willing to do the same?' To which, happily, the people replied 'God save Queen Elizabeth'. After which the trumpets sounded.

The Queen had already subscribed the Declaration, prescribed by Act of Parliament, on 4 November 1952, but she now took and subscribed the Coronation Oath, administered by the Archbishop. She swore to govern not only the peoples of the United Kingdom, but also those of Canada, Australia, New Zealand, the Union of South Africa, Pakistan, Ceylon and her other territories and possessions. She swore to cause 'Law and Justice, in Mercy, to be executed' and

to 'maintain in the United Kingdom the Protestant Reformed Religion'.

The bible was next presented to the Queen. This provided an opportunity for the Moderator of the Church of Scotland to take a part in the ceremony, for it was he who gave her the bible and said: 'Here is Wisdom; This is the royal Law; These are the lively Oracles of God'. Not only was the participation of the Moderator an innovation, but so was the presentation of the bible at this point in the ceremony. At the coronation of the Queen's parents the bible was presented after the crowning.

After the presentation the Communion Service began, which once started before the Oath was taken. It continued to the Creed after which the Queen knelt at her faldstool and was divested of her crimson robe. She then sat in King Edward's Chair, hidden from the gaze of those present by the canopy held over her by the four Knights of the Garter, clad in their splendid full dress, with white satin breeches, crimson velvet kirtles and dark blue robes and awaited the anointing, the central, sacred and mystical part of the whole ceremony.

King Edward's Chair is the wooden Coronation Chair, made at a cost of a hundred shillings for King Edward I to house the Stone of Destiny on which the Scottish kings had been crowned and which he had removed from Scone Abbey in 1296. A certain mystique has always been attached to this chair as even Cromwell had it removed to Westminster Hall for his installation as Lord Protector.

The blessed oil is kept in a vessel, made by Vyner in 1661, called the Ampulla. It is in the shape of an eagle but it should clearly have been a dove as the rite of anointing is very much connected with the Holy Spirit. For example, in old Russian sacrings the words used are 'this impresses the gift of the Holy Ghost'. The oil is poured into a spoon, the handle of which, Mr Lawrence Tanner asserted, 'is unquestionably of the thirteenth century'. The Archbishop anointed the Queen on the palms of both hands, the breast and the crown of the head. In earlier days sovereigns were anointed additionally between the shoulders, on the points thereof and at the bowings of the arms. The present rubric was used at the coronation of William III and Mary II and presumably at that of William IV, although beneath his robe he wore the uniform of an Admiral of the Fleet, which must have created minor complications. At Queen Victoria's coronation, predictably perhaps, the anointing of the breast was omitted.

After the Archbishop had anointed the Queen he said 'And as Solomon was anointed king by Zadok the priest and Nathan the prophet, so be thou

anointed, blessed and consecrated Queen over the Peoples, whom the Lord thy God hath given thee to rule and govern, In the Name of the Father, and of the Son, and of the Holy Ghost, Amen.'.

The canopy was then borne away and the Queen was dressed in the priestly vestments, a rubric anciently known as the 'Investiture with the Ornaments'. These garments are certainly of a sacerdotal nature, although their significance does not appear to have been greatly appreciated, as various monarchs have dispensed with some of the vestments. The first garment is, in priestly fashion, an alb, known as *Colobium Sindonis*, next comes a dalmatic called the *Supertunica* or Close Pall of cloth of gold, together with the girdle or cincture of like material.

At this point, rather curiously, the investing is halted while the spurs and sword are delivered. Until the coronation of Queen Anne the spurs were buckled onto the sovereign's heels and then removed so as not to cause an accident. At Queen Anne's coronation and thereafter the sovereign's heels were touched with the spurs, except at the coronations of Queen Victoria and the present Queen, when the spurs were presented to the sovereign and accepted by touching them.

Thereafter Lord Salisbury delivered the Sword of State to the Lord Chamberlain and in return received a lighter sword, known as the Jewelled Sword in a scabbard. This splendid ceremonial sword was made for the Coronation of George IV at a cost of £6000. It was received by the Archbishop, who, with the other bishops, delivered it to the Queen, saying: 'Receive this kindly Sword, brought now from the Altar of God, and delivered to you by the hands of us the Bishops and servants of God, though unworthy. With this Sword do justice, stop the growth of iniquity, protect the Holy Church of God, help and defend widows and orphans, restore the things that are gone to decay, maintain the things that are restored, punish and reform what is amiss, and confirm what is in good order . . .'

Had the Queen been a King the sword would have been girt about her but as it was she received it in her hands and then offered it, in its scabbard at the Altar, rendering to God what God had entrusted to her. Lord Salisbury then redeemed the sword from the Dean of Westminster for 100 shillings and thereafter carried it naked before the Sovereign during the remainder of the service.

The ancient ceremony of investing the sovereign with the armils or bracelets then took place. This, as I have mentioned, had not been done since before the

coronation of Charles I, although a new pair of armils were made by Vyner for Charles II's coronation. At Charles I's coronation the stole became confused with the armils as the Ceremonial states: 'Then is the Armil put about his neck and tied to the boughts of his arms, the Archbishop saying: "Receive the Bracelets of sinceritie and wisdom as a token of God's embracing".' We put matters right in 1953, the bracelets being first put on the Queen's wrists, with words similar to those quoted and then the Stole Royal and cope called the 'Robe Royal or Pall of cloth of gold', were put upon the Queen by the Dean of Westminster assisted by the Mistress of the Robes.

The Queen was now attired 'like as a Busshop should say masse', symbolic of the divinity which hedges kings, or, to quote from *The Vicar of Bray*:

> 'Kings are by God appointed
> And damned are those who dare resist,
> Or touch the Lord's Anointed'.

Thus consecrated and attired she was ready to receive the symbols of sovereignty, the significance of most of which has already been detailed. Firstly, she received and returned the Orb, then the 'Ring of kingly dignity, and the seal of Catholic Faith . . .' known as the 'Wedding Ring of England' was placed on the fourth finger of her right hand. Here the Queen was luckier than Queen Victoria because Queen Victoria's ring had been made to fit her little finger but the Archbishop insisted on forcing it onto her fourth finger, thus displaying his ignorance of the ancient rubrics which designate no particular finger. According to Charles Greville the ring could only be removed after the ceremony by soaking the royal finger in iced water. Before the coronation of James II the various items of regalia were blessed and consecrated, but, as he was a Roman Catholic, he was uneasy about his regalia being hallowed by clerics he deemed heretical, and so the custom was discontinued. This is sad, as the blessing of the ring strongly reflected the religious mysticism attached to monarchy. 'Blesse O Lord' the rubric ran 'and sanctifie this Ring and send downe upon it thie holy Spirrit, that thy servant wearing it may be sealed with the Ring of faith, and by the power of the Highest be preserved from sin. And let all the blessings which are found in holy Scriptures plentifully descend upon him, that whatsoever he shall sanctify may be holy, and whatsoever he shall blesse may be blessed.'

Next were delivered the Sceptre with the Cross and, into the Queen's left hand, the Rod with the Dove.

At this point I cannot do better than to quote from the Ceremonial, for it needs no comment telling all in words of formal dignity and immemorial grandeur, which would make any remarks of mine sadly prosaic.

> Then the Queen still sitting in King Edward's Chair, the Archbishop, assisted with other Bishops, shall come from the Altar: the Dean of Westminster shall bring the Crown, and the Archbishop taking it of him shall reverently put it upon the Queen's head. At the sight whereof the people, with loud and repeated shouts, shall cry: GOD SAVE THE QUEEN. The Princes and Princesses, the Peers and Peeresses shall put on their coronets and caps, and the Kings of Arms their crowns and the trumpets shall sound and by a signal given, the great guns at the Tower shall be shot off.

The acclamation ceasing, the Archbishop shall go on, and say: 'God crown you with a crown of glory and righteousness that having a right faith and manifold fruit of good work, you may obtain a crown of an everlasting kingdom by the gift of him whose kingdom endureth for ever.'

Thereafter followed the solemn blessing and the enthroning or inthronization as it used to be called. This ceremony of lifting the monarch up and placing him upon a throne is of ancient, pagan origin. The Queen moved in majesty from King Edward's chair, the place of sacring and coronation to a throne set high upon a scaffold (which is simply a dais) between the transepts and facing the high altar, 'the seat and state of royal and imperial dignity'. It is the lineal descendant of the shield upon which primitive kings were carried and tossed in the air. It is recorded that King Grunbald of Burgundy did a 'Humpty-Dumpty' and crashed to the ground; today the ceremony is, happily, much more dignified.

Once enthroned the Queen was ready to receive the homage of the peers. Until 1902 the homage ceremony must, for some of those present, have provided an opportunity for them to relieve themselves and have, as Pooh said, 'a little something', but for others it was an endurance test of the highest order. The reason was that every spiritual and temporal peer present had to ascend the steps of the throne, do their fealty or homage by removing their coronets, kneeling before the sovereign, placing their hands between his and pronouncing the words (in the case of a temporal peer) 'I . . . do become your liege man of life and limb, and of earthly worship; and faith and truth I will bear unto you, to live and die, against all manner of folks. So help me God'. The peer then rose, touched the crown, kissed the sovereign's cheek and retired backwards down the steps. At King Edward VII's coronation this feudal ceremony was drastically curtailed as only the senior peer of each degree did homage, the others of his degree removing their coronets, kneeling in their places and pronouncing the words of homage. Poor Edward VI must have been a particularly patient child (he was nine years old when he was crowned) as every peer did homage kissing his cheek and then his foot 'and so did their homage a pretty time'. After all the peers had done their homage, they knelt, held up their hands and said together 'We offer to sustain You and your Crown with our lives and lands and goods against all the world' which was rather touching and might well have been repeated at subsequent coronations.

At Queen Victoria's coronation, the peers kissed her hand, rather than her cheek. This they also did at the Queen's coronation, except for the Royal Dukes, who did homage separately and kissed the Queen's cheek.

In 1952 the Duke of Norfolk did homage for and with the dukes; the Marquess of Huntley (Lord Winchester, the senior Marquess being unable to attend) did homage for the marquesses, the Earl of Shrewsbury, the premier Earl not having a senior title, did homage for the earls; the Viscount of Arbuthnott did it for the viscounts and Baron Mowbray, Segrave and Stourton for the barons.

That the Scottish Viscount of Arbuthnott did homage caused a little heartache. The premier Viscount was, and is, Viscount Hereford, but he was a minor in 1953, not becoming twenty-one until five months after the coronation. Although there were precedents for minors doing homage – the age was reduced to twenty for George IV's coronation and the Prince of Wales did homage in 1911, having just celebrated his seventeenth birthday – the Earl Marshal ruled against Lord Hereford participating. The next senior Viscount was Lord Falkland, but he wrote to say that he was too old and unwell to attend, so the third senior, Lord Arbuthnott was chosen. Even then it was not plain sailing as the official *Peer's Roll* described him as Viscount Arbuthnott but the Lord Lyon King of Arms, the senior Scottish Herald, told us in unequivocal terms that he should be styled the Viscount of Arbuthnott. Lord Lyon won the day and his Lordship was accorded the preposition in his style.

Before even the Duke of Edinburgh did homage, the Archbishop of Canterbury and the other bishops in their places did their fealty, although technically the Duke has precedence above the Archbishop and bishops rank between viscounts and barons. The reason is that the Church is the First Estate of the Realm, coming before the Lords and Commons. Their submission to the Sovereign is called fealty rather than homage, because they do not swear to become liege men of life and limb, but to be 'faithful and true'. This all goes back to feudal days when

The Duke of Edinburgh kneeling with his hands between the Queen's, doing his homage at the coronation in 1953.

those who held lands of the king did homage for those lands. The spiritual peers were in a rather different situation and this is still reflected in the words of their fealty.

All great ceremonies bring lumps to throats and tears to eyes, and so they should, but the homage is the one part of the coronation ceremony which has captured the sentiment of both kings and journalists. In his account of the coronation the late Godfrey Wynne played heavily on the Duke of Edinburgh kissing his wife's cheek. Even George V wrote in his diary 'I nearly broke down when dear David (the Prince of Wales, later Edward VIII and Duke of Windsor) came to do homage to me, as it reminded me so much of when I did the same thing to beloved Papa, he did it so well. Darling May (Queen Mary) looked lovely and it was indeed a comfort to me to have her by my side'.

The homage has not always been so reverential. At

William IV's coronation the Tories and Whigs cheered their leaders when they came forward to do their homage; indeed, when Lord Brougham and Vaux, the Whig Lord Chancellor, moved towards the Throne, Members of Parliament 'rising *en masse*, waved hats, handkerchiefs and programmes'. One of the Queen's Ladies in Waiting observed that the Commons behaved like 'unruly schoolboys'. Times have not changed in this respect, but, at least, during the Queen's coronation, the faithful Commons' behaviour was impeccable.

Had there been a Queen Consort, she would have been crowned by the Archbishop of York after the homage. The ceremony is similar to the coronation of the sovereign. The Consort kneels for anointing, four peeresses holding a canopy over her. She next receives a ring, is crowned and finally handed her sceptre and her rod with a dove. The Consort is then led to her throne, making an obeisance to her husband.

But let us return to the Queen's coronation. As the consorts of queens regnant are not crowned, the Communion Service, which replaced the old Roman Catholic Mass, began immediately after the homage. To the strains of 'All people that on earth do dwell' the Queen descended from her throne and went to the altar where she delivered her crown, sceptre and rod to the Lord Chamberlain. After the hymn she knelt at her faldstool and offered the bread and wine for the Communion, followed by her oblation which consisted of a pall or altar-cloth, and an ingot of gold, weighing one pound. Until Edward VII's coronation, this oblation was made after the Recognition and a second oblation was made before the Communion. Perhaps the change was made to avoid what happened at William IV's coronation at which, when the time for the second oblation came, the King said to the Archbishop, 'I have not got anything, I will send it to you tomorrow'.

The oblations made, the Duke of Edinburgh joined the Queen and the Communion Service proceeded. When it was ended the Queen received her crown and sceptres and returned to her throne for the singing of the *Gloria* and the blessing. Then, while the *Te Deum Laudamus* was being sung, the Queen retired to St Edward's Chapel, which is directly behind the High Altar. There facilities were provided for her to powder her nose and she also divested herself of the regalia and the Robe Royal, being revested in the robe of purple velvet. St Edward's Crown was laid upon the altar and the Queen received the Imperial State Crown; the Archbishop handed her the Sceptre with the Cross and the Orb and thus arrayed she left the chapel and joined the procession which had been formed up and was waiting to walk slowly back through the choir and down the nave to the west door.

The Imperial State Crown really represents St Edward's Crown; it was made in 1838 by Rundell and Bridge, the jewellers, and is more comfortable to wear as well as being more elegant and resplendent than St Edward's Crown. It contains many notable and historic gems. In the cross at the top of the crown is a sapphire believed to have belonged to St Edward the Confessor; in the front is the Black Prince's Ruby (really red spinel or Bolas ruby) which was given to the Prince by Pedro the Cruel, King of Castile and Leon in 1367 and is said to have been worn by Henry V in his helmet at the battle of Agincourt; below the intersection of the arches hang four great pearls which were probably ear-rings of Queen Elizabeth I and in 1911 was added the second largest portion of the Cullinan diamond weighing 317 carats. The largest portion (530 carats and with seventy-four facets) is in the Sceptre with the Cross.

Once the procession had returned to the Annexe, the royal party retired for a snack and a rest before joining the outside procession back to Buckingham Palace, by way of Whitehall, Pall Mall, St James's Street, Piccadilly, the East Carriage Drive, Oxford Street, Regent Street, Haymarket, Cockspur Street and the Mall. Even the rain did not seem to damp the enthusiasm of the crowds or the stamina of those taking part in the two-mile long procession or that of the 15,000 servicemen lining the route. In the procession itself were 10,000 servicemen, 2500 coming from the Commonwealth and Colonies. There were also twenty-seven bands processing and a further twenty were stationed at points along the route.

The Queen left the Abbey just before 3 p.m. One hour and 40 minutes and 5 miles and 250 yards later, she was back at the Palace to acknowledge the cheers of her damp, but loyal subjects.

So ended what was probably the most dignified and dramatic coronation the country has ever known, a ceremony seen by countless millions, thanks to the magic of the television screen.

Chapter 5

The Sovereign in Parliament

The expression 'The Queen in Parliament' refers to the Queen's constitutional position as part and parcel of the machinery of government. Mention has been made of some of the Queen's prerogatives, such as her right to appoint the Prime Minister, but not of her connexion with day-to-day government, which is two-fold: consultative and ceremonial.

Until the reign of Edward VIII the Prime Minister had the tedious chore of writing daily to the Sovereign in order to inform him of the affairs of the Cabinet and of what went on in the House of Commons. This was abolished by Edward VIII, so Prime Ministers have reason to know of and be grateful for one of the few changes made during that King's brief reign. The Sovereign is still kept informed of everything that goes on, but often it is simply a question of an informal chat with the Prime Minister, or other responsible Minister. Herein lies one of the continuing merits of the monarchy, for governments may come and go and new young Ministers still wet behind the ears, be appointed, but the monarch remains *in situ*, rather like a permanent confessor and advisor. By the very nature of the job, the Sovereign must increase in wisdom and understanding. Who has met so many people, travelled so far, seen so much, followed the affairs of State so closely as the Queen? Can anyone feel the devotion and love of the country that the Queen must feel? Can anyone long for and work for peace, harmony and careful and wise government as passionately as the Queen? And there she is, ideally situated to do her best to lead by advising and by putting at the disposal of her Ministers, the value of her incomparable experience. It would be a foolish sovereign to dictate to a Minister what he should do, but an equally foolish Minister to disregard the sovereign's advice as to how and when to do something.

In her formal connexion with Parliament, the roles are reversed. The Queen, instead of advising her Ministers, is advised by them and traditionally acts on their advice. This is nicely symbolized in the recital of an Act of Parliament which runs: 'Be it enacted by The Queen's Most Excellent Majesty, by and with the advice and consent of the Lords Spiritual and Temporal, and Commons in this present Parliament assembled, and by the authority of the same as follows . . .'. Before a Bill, which has been read three times in both Houses of Parliament, can become law, it must receive the Royal Assent. Contrary to popular belief, the Queen does not sign each Bill. What actually happens is that when a Bill has been passed, an official at the Palace of Westminster called the Clerk of the Crown prepares a Commission by which the Queen will appoint Commissioners to convey her Royal Assent to the Bill, or, more often, to a number of Bills, detailed in the Commission. The Queen then signs, not the Bills, but the Commission, naming the Commissioners, who are peers and Privy Counsellors; the Lord Chancellor then affixes the Great Seal to the Commission.

At a sitting of the House of Lords the Lord Chancellor and the other Commissioners who have been appointed sit in front of the Throne, which is called the Cloth of Estate and symbolizes the Queen's presence. The Gentleman Usher of the Black Rod is then ordered to summon the Commons to the Bar of the House of Lords which is opposite the Throne at the other end of the Chamber. The Speaker and a deputation composed of senior Ministers and of members of other parties comes to the bar.

The Clerk of the Crown then reads the name of each Bill and the Clerk of the Parliaments gives the Royal Assent verbally, saying, 'La Reine le veult' (the Queen wishes it). Of course, the Queen could attend

Henry VIII proceeding to Parliament in 1512. The Cap of Maintenance and Sword of State are carried before him. Garter King of Arms walks behind the Lords Spiritual.

in person and give the Royal Assent, as her father once did in the Canadian Parliament in 1939, but no sovereign has attended the House for this purpose for a very long time.

Another ceremony where the Sovereign is notionally but not physically present in Parliament is that which is enacted when a newly created peer is formally introduced into the House of Lords and takes his seat. However, before describing this ceremony something must be said about the members of the House of Lords, the peers of the realm.

Technically, a peer is one who is an equal, but actually, the peers are neither equal to the sovereign, nor to each other, although, in formal documents, the Queen addresses peers as 'cousin'. A duke, for example, is addressed by the Crown as 'Our right trusty and right entirely beloved cousin'. Lower down the scale, this salutation becomes less effusive, a

viscount being but 'Our right trusty and well-beloved cousin'. It can be said, however, that the Queen and her peers form an Estate of the Realm and so to that extent they are equal.

There are two sorts of peers, Lord Spiritual and Lords Temporal. The former are the archbishops and bishops and, until the Reformation, also the abbots and the Lord Prior of the Order of St John. The latter are, in order of seniority, the dukes, marquesses, earls, viscounts and barons. Confusion often arises because all except dukes are informally addressed as 'Lord'. For example, although one would address an envelope to 'The Marquess of Bath', or even more grandly to 'The Most Honourable The Marquess of Bath', one would refer to him in speech and in the salutation to the letter simply as 'Lord Bath'.

To complicate matters further, there are three varieties of baron: hereditary barons created by

66

patent, hereditary barons created by writ, and Life barons, among which I have included Lords of Appeal in Ordinary for they are, to all intents and purposes, Life peers, although they are created pursuant to the Appellate Jurisdiction Acts, rather than to the Life Peerages Act.

Hereditary barons created by patent are like peers in other degrees of the peerage. They are created by Letters Patent under the Great Seal, to the end that they and the heirs male of their bodies lawfully begotten, or to be begotten, may have, hold, and enjoy the state, degree, style, dignity and title of a baron and have, hold and possess a seat, place and voice in Parliament. Unless otherwise stated in the patent, succession is in order of male primogeniture, known as 'tail male'.

The document is called Letters Patent because it is an open, public Act of the Sovereign, the Great Seal

hanging beneath it, from a cord, and not sealing it as if in an envelope. The word 'patent', from the Latin *patere*, means 'to be open'.

Baronies by writ go back to the early days of the Great Council when men were summoned as 'Lord of So-and-So' to serve and attend the Council on a particular occasion. In the seventeenth century it was held that if a person in receipt of a writ summoning him to Parliament took his seat therein he had been created an hereditary peer. As Lord Coke puts it the 'delivery of the Writ . . . maketh (a man) not noble . . . until he sit in Parliament and thereby his blood is ennobled to him and his heirs lineal'.

The main difference between a barony by writ and a barony by patent is that while the inheritance of the latter is confined to the legitimate heirs male of the body of the grantee, in the case of the former, it is deemed that, in default of heirs male, heirs female may

Lord Castle, with his supporting peers and Richmond Herald, before his Introduction in the House of Lords in 1974.

succeed. But there is a snag. In English law, there were no rights of primogeniture among women; thus if a baron by writ died leaving four daughters, who was to succeed, the eldest having no seniority over the youngest? It is held that in these circumstances, the peerage becomes abeyant until the Crown, advised by the House of Lords, itself advised by a Committee of the House called the Committee for Privileges, terminates the abeyance in favour of one of the co-heirs. In practice, although there are many such baronies abeyant and likely to remain so, public policy not being in favour of terminating abeyancies, few hereditary barons and baronesses by writ actually have a seat in the Lords.

Before the Act of Union with Scotland in 1707 there was a separate Scottish peerage. As Scottish law is different from English law, there is no abeyancy in Scotland. If there is more than one heiress to a peerage created not in 'tail male', but to 'heirs whomsoever', the eldest succeeds. The result of this is that there is a number of Scottish peeresses in their own right. Until the Peerage Act 1963, neither English Peeresses by Writ, nor hereditary Scottish Peeresses could sit in the House of Lords, but now they all are able to do so. In fact, there are less than twenty hereditary peeresses in their own right, of whom one is an Italian.

Finally, there are Life barons and baronesses, created pursuant to the Life Peerages Act 1958, or the

Appellate Jurisdiction Acts 1876 and 1887. Such peers are in every way the same as other peers except that their titles are not descendible to their heirs. There is a Royal Warrant which states that the wives and widows of Life peers and the sons and daughters of Life peers and peeresses 'shall be treated for their style, rank, dignity and precedence' in the same way as those of hereditary peers. Since Mr John Morrison was created Baron Margadale in 1965, neither a Conservative nor a Socialist administration has recommended the Queen to create other than Life peerages.

The Lords Spiritual are now a very diminished body. The Archbishops of Canterbury and York have seats in the House of Lords, as do the Bishops of London, Durham and Winchester. Of the thirty-eight remaining Anglican Diocesans, the senior twenty-one, by date of appointment, also have seats. The only bishop who never sits is the Bishop of Sodor and Man, as he is a member of the Legislative Council of the Isle of Man.

The Lords Spiritual still sit to the right of the Throne. This side of the House is called the Spiritual Side, but as these peers are so few in number, they are joined by the Government of the day.

When the Prime Minister has advised the Queen to create someone a Life peer, that person having agreed to accept the honour, the first thing that happens is that he (obviously, the procedure is the same for a woman) is asked to consult with Garter King of Arms regarding the title by which he wishes to be known. There are two elements of the title: the substantive title and the territorial title.

Many Life peers wish to retain their surnames and use them as their titles and this is possible where there can be no confusion with other peers. Thus, Sir Geoffrey Bourne, there being no other Lord Bourne, became Baron Bourne, of Atherstone in the County of Warwick. His substantive title, that under which he will appear in the official Peers' Roll and be styled and designated, is Bourne. The rest is the compulsory territorial addition which is not used. Sir Ian Fraser was not so lucky as there was already a Lord Fraser. This meant that the only way in which he could retain his name was by adding to it, so he became Baron Fraser of Lonsdale, of Regent's Park in the County of London.

Once a title has been chosen, a Royal Warrant, signed by the Queen, directs that the Letters Patent be prepared. When this has passed the Great Seal the new peer is truly a peer and receives a printed Writ of Summons to attend Parliament. In this the Queen commands him 'upon the faith and allegiance by which you are bound to Us . . . (waiving all excuses) you be personally present at Our . . . Parliament with Us and with the Prelates Nobles and Peers of Our . . . Kingdom to treat and give your counsel . . . And this as you regard Us and Our honour and safety and defence of the . . . Kingdom and Church . . . in nowise do you omit . . .'.

However, as a new peer, he cannot sit in Parliament until he has been officially introduced into the House. In order to arrange for this, the first thing he must do is to find two peers of like degree (that is barons or baronesses) who will act as his sponsors, or supporters. A day is then appointed for the ceremony, which traditionally takes place immediately after prayers and before the business of the day. This is usually at 2.35 p.m.

The officers who officiate on this occasion are the Gentleman Usher of the Black Rod and Garter King of Arms. As there have been so many creations of Life peers in recent years, Garter (as he is always known) has often appointed a deputy to act for him and, as I have so acted on many occasions, I shall describe the ceremony from a personal, herald's point of view.

On the day of the Introduction, I put on my Royal Household uniform and am collected from the College of Arms by a Government motor-car. I arrive at the House at about mid-day and see that all the props are ready: robes and hats for the new peer and his sponsors, Garter's tabard, sceptre and collar of SS (an ancient royal badge, composed of linked silver-gilt esses, worn by, among others, the Kings and Heralds of Arms), the Letters Patent and the dummy which will be used for the ceremony.

Customarily, the new peer gives a lunch party to which are bidden his sponsors, Black Rod, Garter or his deputy, the Clerk of the Parliaments and any others he sees fit to invite. This enables those taking part to get to know each other and helps to calm 'first night nerves'. I have been frequently surprised to find how nervous hardened campaigners are when faced with the ordeal of this simple ten-minute ceremony. The first peer I ever introduced was Lady Violet Bonham-Carter who had been created Baroness Asquith of Yarnbury in 1964. We were each equally uneasy and I remember her asking my advice as to whether I thought it better for us to drink wine or water with our lunch. Being a firm believer in using water principally for washing in, I replied that I thought wine in moderation might calm our nerves. It was a dry, not over-fruity Moselle and it did the trick. We romped through the ceremony in fine style.

I not only regard this traditional lunch as an opportunity for Black Rod and myself to put the performers at their ease, but also as a way in which the new peer can say 'thank you' because the Standing

Orders of the House of Lords inhibit him from giving any pecuniary reward and there is no doubt that officiating at an Introduction takes a large slice out of the working day.

Lunch over, we retire to the robing room, which is usually a Committee Room called The Moses Room. Here the three peers select hats from the assorted collection provided by the House. If they are barons they take cocked hats, if baronesses a velour tricorn, specially approved by the Queen when women were admitted to the House, for use at Introductions. The present Black Rod, Sir David House, likes the peers to rehearse in their robes, which is sensible as they take a little getting used to, but this is a recent innovation. Black Rod and I then take them through their paces in the actual Chamber, one of the Clerks taking the part of the Lord Chancellor. A couple of rehearsals is usually sufficient, although, I am told, Lord Olivier insisted on four.

After the rehearsals, I put on the tabard, my coat-tails being hooked up behind me so as not to hang demoniacally below the heavy velvet, gold embroidered tabard. The peers are already enveloped in their robes of scarlet cloth trimmed with two rows of white fur edged with gold lace. Usually some photographs are taken before we form up in single file to await Black Rod's summons.

I stand in front with Garter's sceptre in my right hand and the dummy Patent in my left. The reason we use a dummy is because the actual Patent is a beautifully engrossed and illuminated document which is kept in a sort of red attaché case. From a ceremonial point of view, it certainly looks better for it to be represented by a scroll of vellum with a representation of the Great Seal hanging from it. Behind me is the junior sponsor then the new peer, holding his Writ of Summons (if he has remembered to bring it; I remember one peer who forgot it and a piece of plain paper was hastily produced, folded to look like the writ). Behind him is the senior sponsor. Peers carry their cocked hats in their left hands against their left breasts; peeresses wear their tricorns and never remove them. The Queen, when she approved this procedure, appreciated that it is not always as easy for women to don and doff their headgear as it is for men.

If they wish, the Earl Marshal, robed and carrying his baton and the Lord Great Chamberlain, also robed and bearing his white staff, may walk behind me, but within my memory they have only ever been present at the Introduction of the Prince of Wales.

The closed-circuit television set tells us how things are going outside – 'Lord Chancellor's Procession – Prayers – Prayers Over; Lord Chancellor on the Woolsack'. Then, in a moment, Black Rod comes to the door of the robing room, wearing black knee-breeches, cut away coat and decorations, and carrying his long black rod, the symbol of his office.

'Proceed', he exclaims and then leads the little procession slowly to the Peers' Lobby. As we enter an usher cries 'Hats off strangers!', and we wheel right and move towards the doors of the House, which are flung open as we approach. The Lord Chancellor is sitting robed on the Woolsack, a Tricorn on his full bottomed wig. The clerks sit at their table in the centre of the House, also robed and wigged and on either side, on the scarlet benches, their Lordships and Ladyships sit, loll and sprawl, the latter tending to desport themselves more decorously than the former. We all bow (just an inclination of the head, which is the court bow) to the Cloth of Estate at the bar of the House, one after the other, then again, as we move down the temporal side of the House towards the Woolsack, we bow at the table (about half way down) and at the Judges' Woolsacks (just before the Lord Chancellor's). When we reach the Lord Chancellor, the new peer goes down on one knee and presents his writ to the Chancellor while I, standing just behind his right shoulder hand him the Letters Patent. These the Lord Chancellor touches as a symbol of acceptance and they are then taken by the Reading Clerk. The procession now reverses and returns to the table. I walk around the back of the Woolsack, up the Spiritual Side of the House and station myself behind the Clerks' bench. The Reading Clerk reads the Letters Patent and then the Writ of Summons. The new Peer takes the Oath of Allegiance to 'The Queen Her Heirs and Successors'. If he has conscientious objections to taking a Christian oath, he may make an affirmation of loyalty. If he is Jewish he takes the Oath of the Old Testament and may conform to the Jewish custom by assuming his hat when doing so. A Scotsman I introduced told me that Scots held the Good Book aloft when they took an Oath. I am sure he was right, but in any case, he was not the sort of Scot with whom you argue the toss, so he took the Oath in the way he wanted.

Once the Oath has been taken, the new peer signs the Peer's Roll (literally a large roll of vellum membranes stuck together), picks up his hat and the procession is resumed. At this point, I lead it back along the Spiritual Side of the House, below the bar and up the steps to the back to the Barons' Bench on the Temporal Side. Again we all bow seriatim to the

Opposite: Queen Elizabeth the Queen Mother and the Prince of Wales walking in procession to St George's Chapel, Windsor, for the annual service of the Order of the Garter in 1979.

Cloth of Estate as we cross the House. The three peers line up in the back bench and I stand facing them by the bench below, feeling, and looking I dare say, rather like a conductor; but, in a way, that is what I am at this point in the ceremony. In a stage whisper I issue the following commands: 'Sit down – put on your hats – rise – take off your hats and bow to the Chancellor – put on your hats – sit down – rise – take off your hats . . .' and so on three times. After the third bow I have to try to remember to alter the command and say 'keep your hats off and follow me'. I then lead them down the gangway of the floor of the House. Black Rod rejoins us and we walk down the Temporal Side of the House, past the Lord Chancellor and out of the Chamber. As the new peer passes the Lord Chancellor he shakes his hand and the House growls its approval.

The three bows to the Lord Chancellor (he acknowledges them by removing his tricorn) are not court bows like those to the Cloth of Estate, but deep obeisances. No one knows why there are three bows but Sir Anthony Wagner and Mr J.C. Sainty, in an interesting article on this ceremony, published in *Archaeologia*, point out that the numbers three and nine have been regarded as sacred numbers among Indo-European peoples from Vedic to Christian times. The number three of course acquired an additional symbolism among Christians, because of their Trinitarian theology.

This ceremony of Introduction is of comparatively recent origin, having first been used in 1621. There is some reason to believe that it was devised by Thomas Earl of Arundel, who had been restored to the office of Earl Marshal in that year; certainly, it is the kind of task which might well have fallen to the Earl Marshal as a principal ceremonial officer of the Crown. It is really a sort of amalgam of two ceremonies which previously took place, the Ceremonial Investiture of a new peer by the sovereign and his being placed in his seat in the House of Lords by Garter King of Arms. The former ceremony, that of investiture took place wherever the king happened to be, but the latter ceremony always took place in Parliament.

It is worth describing these ceremonies briefly as they explain, to some extent, how the present ceremony came into being. The Letters Patent creating a peer expressly state that they are sufficient for 'dignifying, investing and really ennobling' the new peer 'without any investiture, rites, ornaments or ceremonies . . . due and accustomed . . .'. It is with investiture that I shall treat firstly.

Opposite: *The Queen wearing her bonnet as Sovereign of the Order of the Thistle.*

Until 1621 the newly created peer was summoned to appear before the sovereign for his formal investiture. The actual ceremony varied a little, according to the rank of the newly ennobled. If he were an earl, marquess or duke, he was robed before being led into the presence of the sovereign, if he were a baron or viscount, he simply wore a kirtle. The new peer, between two sponsors was led into the royal presence by the heralds, Garter King of Arms carrying the Letters Patent. After him came various peers bearing such insignia as might be required; then there followed the new peer and his supporters. As they approached the sovereign, they made three obeisances. Then the new peer knelt before the sovereign between his sponsors, while Garter handed the Letters Patent to the Lord Chamberlain, who handed them to a Secretary to read. At certain moments in the reading of the Patent the Secretary paused while the sovereign performed such action as had been described. For example, the Letters Patent creating Edward Courtenay Earl of Devon recite '. . . by girding of a sword we have marked, invested and really ennobled' (here the sword of the earldom was put about him) 'and a cap of honour and dignity, also a circle of gold on his head we place' (the cap and coronet were here imposed upon his head) 'to have and hold the name, status, style, title, honour and dignity of Earl of Devon . . .'.

Once the new peer had been invested he was able to take his seat in Parliament and this he did in another ceremony conducted by Garter King of Arms, but which, before the creation of the office of Garter in 1415, was probably the Marshal's responsibility, hence his present right to take part in Introductions if he so wishes. For officiating at this ceremony 'Gartier demandith to have a reward for . . . just entrees and thordering of their setes and registring of their names and armes'. This reward has now become a lunch.

Today, a new peer signs the Roll and the Secretary who reads the Patent is the Reading Clerk, but it is not difficult to see how the Earl of Arundel, if indeed it were he, devised the present ceremony.

In 1964 some noble lords tried to prune even this comparatively exiguous ritual, but their motion was easily defeated. If the Queen still ennobles people and if such people enter into a new estate and become members of the High Court of Parliament, they and everyone else wish to see this done formally, solemnly and in the context of history. It has nothing to do with party politics (as the vote in 1964 eloquently testified, many Labour peers voting against change). It is a question of established, constitutional, ceremonial behaviour. Such things should be done properly, or they should not be done at all.

Opposite: *The Queen in the Irish State Coach, bought in Dublin by Queen Victoria in 1852, on her way to the State Opening of Parliament in 1973.*

The only time the Sovereign is physically present in Parliament is at the State Opening of Parliament, which normally takes place once a year. This is one of the state ceremonies which the heralds, as officers under the Earl Marshal arrange and attend. In fact, one of the heralds usually makes all the arrangements which tend to vary little from year to year. To breathe a little life into this ceremony, I will describe one of the many occasions on which I have participated, from an essentially personal point of view.

On the morning of the State Opening, I dressed in a white shirt and black tights, then, suitably covered by an ordinary suit, made my way to the College of Arms. Here I donned my black breeches, sword in shoulder sling, scarlet coatee and buckled, patent-leather shoes. At 9.30 a.m. a Government motor-car arrived to take me and two of my colleagues to the House of Lords. We drove along the Embankment and drew up at the Peers' Entrance to the Houses of Parliament where the privileged (comparatively) few were already queuing up to be admitted to the Royal Gallery in order to view part of the proceedings. In and around Parliament Square the crowds were already beginning to assemble to watch the arrival and departure of the Queen, the Imperial State Crown and members of the Royal Family.

Scouts opened the doors of the motorcar and we stiffly, our uniforms not being conducive to excessive physical activity, eased ourselves out. I walked through the cloakroom, where every peer has his own coat hook, designated by his title, and then up the splendid staircase, decorated with armorial bearings, the latest being those of the late Lord Selwyn-Lloyd, the last Speaker of the House of Commons, who became a Life peer when he retired. I passed on down the passage into the Princes' Chamber, which is the ante-room which lies between the House of Lords and the Royal Gallery. The latter is a wide gallery of about the same dimensions as the House itself. On this occasion, behind barriers on either side, raised platforms are constructed on which the guests stand to watch the procession, which moves from the Queen's Robing Room at the far end of the Gallery down to the Princes' Chamber and so into the House itself, and then back, after the Gracious Speech. There are also some boxes, which are roped off and in which chairs are provided for the guests of certain eminent officials, such as the Earl Marshal and the Lord Great Chamberlain.

I passed quickly through the Princes' Chamber, on down the passage, made a right turn at the entrance to the Lords' Library, down another passage lined with calf-bound tomes of legal proceedings, then took a sharp left and arrived at the Committee Room placed at the disposal of the Officers of Arms as a robing room. This is a splendid, dignified room with panoramic views over the river and eastwards to St Paul's. Laid out on tables round the room were our tabards, wands and collars of SS. Tailors, who will later hook and eye and tie us into our royal coats, hover around.

However, there is a good three quarters of an hour before we need augment our sartorial discomfort and so, leaving my hat and cloak by my tabard, I retraced my steps to the Princes' Chamber. Signs of activity are now discernible everywhere. Peers in their Parliament Robes are milling about. Peeresses, who have been lucky in the draw for a strictly limited number of seats are eyeing each other's evening dresses, elaborate hair-dos and tiaras (for it is a tiara occasion). The *Corps Diplomatique* is out in force, resplendent in a variety of uniforms and ceremonial dresses, glittering with exotic Orders and decorations and all looking a little lost; but not for long. The Marshal and Vice-Marshal of the *Corps* and their trained and expert staff are there busy greeting and sorting out the foreign envoys.

After discovering a few friends and acquaintances, disguised in robes, legal wigs and uniforms, I entered the Royal Gallery just as the doors at the end on the right had been opened to admit the public. Some entered bewildered and a little over-awed by the splendour, obviously wondering where to take their stand. Others were clearly old hands and scurried for certain key positions.

The regulations, detailed on the tickets, stated that Ladies should wear 'Day Dress with Hat', with the gloss that they 'are asked to wear small hats in order that all in the Royal Gallery may have the best possible view'. Gentlemen should wear 'Morning or Service Dress or Lounge Suits'. Sadly, formality is becoming more and more a thing of the past; I hope this simply reflects economic trends and not an increasing unawareness of sense of occasion; every year morning coats and elegant dresses become rarer and the general impression conveyed by the crowd in the Royal Gallery is more akin to that of a minor Race Meeting than of the Queen's Court in her Palace of Westminster.

The crowd streamed in, and up and down the wide gangway between the barriers, robed peers, judges, heralds and other functionaries and dignitaries strutted and gossiped. Past and present are telescoped in the timeless ritual and splendour which, at heart, everyone loves and reveres. On this occasion, more than on any other, it becomes apparent that the corner-stone of the edifice of the State is the Sovereign in Parliament – apolitical, impartial, permanent and constitutionally ceremonial. However fiercely the tempests of political antagonism may rage and crises beyond our shores threaten us, as Suez did at the time of the State Opening in 1956, we show a united front to the world, personified by 'Elizabeth the Second . . . of the United Kingdom of Great Britain and Northern Ireland and of Her other Realms and Territories Queen, Head of the Commonwealth and Defender of the Faith'.

At about 10.40 a.m. I returned to our Committee Room, named the Salisbury Room, to be robed. At 10.45 a.m. a dismounted party of the Household Cavalry arrived at the Norman Porch and lined the staircase up which the Queen is to walk; the Life Guards formed up on one side and the Blues and Royals on the other side of the staircase. Two minutes later the Queen's Bodyguard of the Yeoman of the Guard entered the Royal Gallery to take up their stations in front of the barriers, obscuring the view of some of the guests, but looking very splendid in their Tudor uniforms. Then the other Queen's Bodyguard, the Honourable Corps of Gentlemen at Arms, a Bodyguard composed of retired officers, moved into the Princes' Chamber and fanned out in a semi-circle. At the same time, the crown, the Sword of State and the Cap of Maintenance arrived at the Royal Entrance, just beside and at right angles to the Norman Porch, and within minutes were brought under escort into the Royal Gallery. The crown is the Imperial State Crown which I described in the last chapter. The Sword of State is a magnificent two-handed sword, the quillons being in the form of a lion and a unicorn, the supporters of the royal coat of arms. The blade, which is thirty-two inches long, is encased in a scabbard of crimson velvet, decorated with the royal arms and badges. This is the Sovereign's personal sword; the symbol of royal authority. The Cap of Maintenance is a cap of crimson velvet turned up with ermine. It is an ancient symbol of dignity and authority and although it has really been eclipsed by the crown, it is still carried on the end of a pole, at the Opening of Parliament.

While all this was happening, I and my brother officers have been helped into our tabards by the tailors who always attend on such occasions, as it is more or less impossible to hook and eye and tie oneself into one's own tabard. Carrying our wands, or staves of office, we took up our stations in the Princes' Chamber.

As soon as the crown had been safely placed on a table at the far end of the Royal Gallery, we proceeded down the gallery, turned right and took up our places on the staircase in front of the Household Cavalry. Just after 11 o'clock members of the Royal Family attending the Opening arrived at the Norman Porch. They went to the robing room and then walked in procession down the Royal Gallery and into the House of Lords. Normally the only members of the Royal Family to walk in the Queen's procession are the Duke of Edinburgh, the Prince of Wales and Princess Anne, although in 1956, the Duke of Edinburgh being abroad, Princess Margaret accompanied the Queen and walked in the Royal Procession. As it is not customary for the widow of a sovereign to attend, the Queen Mother has not been present at any State Opening.

At seven minutes past eleven, the Lord High Chancellor, wearing his black robe embellished with gold lace, a full bottomed wig and carrying the purse in which the Great Seal should repose, but which actually contains the Queen's Speech, joined the other Great Officers of State at the foot of the staircase.

Faintly in the distance, then growing louder came the sound of cheering, mingled with that of the hooves of many horses. Then the strains of the National Anthem were heard and we knew that the Queen would arrive at the Royal Entrance at any moment, but before that carriages would draw up at the Norman Porch and the Master of the Horse, the Mistress of the Robes and a Lady and a Woman of the Bedchamber would hurry out to be ready for the Queen's arrival.

A fanfare of trumpets sounded. The command 'Household Cavalry – Royal Salute – Carry Swords' rang out and then, walking backwards from the Royal Entrance, appeared the Earl Marshal and the Lord Great Chamberlain, the Marquess of Cholmondeley. The Earl Marshal raised his baton and we turned about to lead the royal party up the staircase.

At the top of the staircase, we moved into the Royal Gallery and took our places in the procession which was forming. The Queen and the Duke of Edinburgh went into the Robing Room. There the Queen put on the Robe of State and the Crown. The robe consists of an ermine cape with a train of crimson velvet, which is lined with ermine and also bordered with ermine and gold lace. It is over eighteen feet long and nearly four feet wide and is carried by four pages, dressed in white breeches and stockings and wearing coats of the royal livery of scarlet and yellow. The Duke of Edinburgh has not so far worn his duke's parliament robe, as do the other royal dukes, and the occasion I am describing was no exception; he escorted the Queen, wearing the uniform of an Admiral of the Fleet.

While the Queen was robing, the procession in the Royal Gallery had formed up. In front were the pursuivants, followed by the heralds. Next came members of the Queen's, Duke of Edinburgh's and Prince of Wales' personal households, flanked by two Serjeants at Arms carrying enormous seventeenth century, silver-gilt maces. Then came the Comptroller and Treasurer of the Household, Mr James Hamilton, and the Right Honourable Walter Harrison. These are political appointments, the holders of which are Assistant Government Whips in the House of Commons. Behind them were the Keeper of the Privy Purse and the Queen's Private Secretary, Clarenceux and Norroy and Ulster Kings of Arms, the Lord Chancellor and the Lord President of the Council, who, on this occasion, was Mr Michael Foot.

Black Rod and Garter King of Arms came next, then the Earl Marshal, who would later be joined by the Lord Great Chamberlain. Finally, there were Field Marshal Lord Carver, who carried the Sword of State, held in a sling because of its great weight, and Lord Peart bearing the Cap of Maintenance, physically a far less onerous task.

The sense of occasion had now gripped everyone

The Earl of Halsbury, Lord High Chancellor, wearing his coronation robe and holding his coronet and Chancellor's purse: a drawing by Byam-Shaw.

and there was complete silence as we waited for the Lord Great Chamberlain to come in and signify to the door keepers that Her Majesty was ready. He entered, signalled with his white wand and the doors opened to reveal the Queen in majesty, swift rays of light shooting from the hundreds of jewels in the crown, her left hand reposing in her husband's right. Behind her came the Prince of Wales followed by the Mistress of the Robes, the Duchess of Grafton, Lady Abergavenny, a Lady of the Bedchamber and Lady Susan Hussey, a Woman of the Bedchamber. Behind them were the Lord Steward, the Master of the Horse, and Gold Stick in Waiting, who, on this occasion, was Field Marshal Sir Gerald Templer, the other Gold Stick being Lord Mountbatten of Burma. They were followed by a Lord in Waiting, the Vice-Admiral of the United Kingdom and the Captains of the Gentlemen at Arms and the Yeoman of the Guard. The latter are political appointments being respectively the Chief Government Whip and Assistant Whip in the House of Lords. When the Labour Government came to power in 1974 a woman, Lady Llewelyn-Davies of Harsoe, for the first time in history became Chief Whip. We all wondered whether a uniform would be invented for her, but in the end she opted for what might be described as a smart, military-style outfit and very handsome she looked in it. The Captains were followed by three Aides-de-Camp, the Gentleman Usher to the Sword of State, the Comptroller of the Lord Chamberlain's Office, the Field Officer in Brigade Waiting, the Lieutenant of the Gentleman at Arms and his opposite number in the Yeoman of the Guard, who bears the ancient title of Clerk of the Cheque and Adjutant.

The Queen advanced to a fanfare of trumpets and as she neared the Earl Marshal and Lord Great Chamberlain, Garter King of Arms waved his sceptre, we all about-turned and moved slowly towards the House of Lords. In the Princes' Chamber the front portion of the procession moved to the left, and we stood in a group near the throne. We then saw the rest of the procession entering through the right-hand door, the Earl Marshal and Lord Great Chamberlain walking backwards before the Sovereign. As the Queen entered the lights of the House, which had been dimmed, were turned up, a theatrical and, so, some might think, a slightly un-British gesture, but none the less effective. The House rose, the Queen ascended the dais and the pages arranged the train of her robe, then she sat down and said 'My Lords, pray

Black Rod knocking on the door of the House of Commons, seeking admission to summon members of the House to the Bar of the House of Lords to hear the Queen's speech.

be seated'. The peeresses did not remain standing; they know that on this occasion they just have to grin and bear being described as lords. The Duke of Edinburgh, who at the beginning of the reign used to sit on a chair, now occupies a throne similar to and next to the Queen's. Prince Charles sat in a chair to the right of the throne and, had Princess Anne been present, she would have sat to the left of the throne, just behind the Lord carrying the Sword of State and in front of the Queen's Ladies.

The Lord Great Chamberlain signalled to Black Rod, who left the Chamber and made his way to the House of Commons. On arrival the doors were closed in his face and he knocked on them three times with his rod. He was then admitted and requested the presence of the Honourable House at the Bar of the House of Lords. In fact, in 1978, the Commons were not ready for him and the usual awkward pause of four minutes was extended to eight, much to everyone's embarrassment. King George VI found this hiatus tiresome as the crown was heavy and he had to sit motionless on the throne while everyone either stared at him, or self-consciously tried to look elsewhere. The King did away with the pause, by

The Queen processing through the Royal Gallery at the opening of Parliament in 1976. She is followed by her Ladies in Waiting and members of the Royal Household.

seeing that Black Rod went off to the Commons as the procession started. In this way, the Commons arrived at the Bar just as the King was seated. The Queen followed suit until 1958 when she reverted to the traditional routine.

At last the Commons, or some of them, arrived at the Bar, led by the Speaker and the Party leaders, their noisy progress through the Peers' Lobby being very audible in the silent Chamber of the Lords. The Lord Chancellor then ascended the steps of the throne, went down on one knee before the Sovereign, who by now had put on her recently acquired spectacles and,

withdrawing the Speech from his purse, handed it to her, then we all held our breath as he walked backwards down the steps, the train of his robe looped over his arm, as this is no easy manoeuvre.

The speech is not of course written by the Queen, but by her Government and outlines its intentions for the next Session. It is no literary masterpiece and I always feel sorry for the Queen having to read the tired clichés as if she had written them herself. The speech always ends with the words 'I pray that the blessing of Almighty God will rest upon your counsels'; this is our cue to hurry out and form up in the

Royal Gallery while the rest of the procession takes its place behind us. At a signal from Garter we moved off down the Gallery, turning right at the end, preparatory to lining the staircase once again. The Queen and her entourage went back into the robing room. When she had been divested of the Crown and Robe she put on the diadem made for George IV and took her leave. We led her down to the Royal Entrance and stood outside in a semi-circle on the steps. The Irish State Coach, bought in Dublin by Queen Victoria in 1852 and drawn by six greys, was waiting. The footmen helped the Queen in, one of them collapsed the steps, the four footmen then jumped up behind, the chocs were removed and, escorted by a Sovereign's escort of the Household Cavalry, the coachman in wig and tricorn hat drove the coach back to Buckingham Palace. The ladies in waiting followed, and then, in a special coach, illuminated by electric light, were placed the crown and the maces, their heads projecting through the windows. This coach followed the royal coach so that the crowds lining the route were able to see, not just the Sovereign, but the perennial symbols of her sovereignty and authority.

Once the crown had left we made our way back to the Salisbury Room, gratefully shed our tabards and then joined the crowd outside the Peers' Entrance.

The Queen is also notionally in Parliament at a number of other ceremonies, such as when approving the election of a new Speaker of the House of Commons. On this occasion Commissioners, robed and seated in front of the throne, inform the Commons, who have been summoned to the Bar, that it is the Sovereign's wish that they elect one of their number to be Speaker. This they do and then, on a day appointed, the Speaker-elect, attended by members of the House of Commons, goes to the House of Lords to seek the Queen's approval. This is always given, just as the privileges claimed for the Commons by the Speaker, especially 'freedom of speech in debate . . . freedom from arrest . . . free access to Her Majesty whenever occasion shall require' are granted.

A Commission of Peers also acts for the Sovereign at the annual prorogation of Parliament, although the Queen could be present, as was her great-great-grandmother, Queen Victoria, in 1855, if she wished. As on other occasions, the Commons are summoned to the Bar of the Lords by Black Rod. Led by the Speaker, they arrive, make three deep obeisances, which the Commissioners return, doffing their hats in an almost theatrical gesture. The Letters Patent appointing the Commissioners are then read and the presiding peer, usually the Lord Chancellor, reads the prorogation speech which, like the speech with which the Queen opens Parliament, is written by the Government. Parliament is then formally prorogued until an agreed date and the Session is at an end.

Some may think these ceremonies unnecessary and so, in a way, they are. On the other hand, they are a safeguard; while they exist and are an accepted part of the constitution, that constitution and the rights and freedoms of the people cannot easily be eroded by evil men. It is important to keep the outward forms if the inner substance is to remain intact.

Chapter 6

The Prince of Wales

There is a common and understandable misconception that the eldest son of the sovereign is automatically Prince of Wales, and that, as such, he bears the badge consisting of three ostrich feathers enfiled by a coronet and with a scroll inscribed 'Ich dien' (I serve) – 'The Prince of Wales' feathers'.

Such is not the case. The title Prince of Wales is conferred by the sovereign by a formal document under the Great Seal, in much the same way as a peerage is created. However, it is only ever bestowed upon the heir apparent to the throne, who is automatically Duke of Cornwall and, in Scotland, Duke of Rothesay, Earl of Carrick, Baron Renfrew, Lord of the Isles and Great Steward of Scotland. Obviously, it is for this reason and because most, although not all, sovereigns have bestowed the title on their eldest sons, that it is generally thought that the principate is attached to the other titles.

In the same way, because the heir apparent is usually also Prince of Wales, by which title he is known, as it takes precedence over his inherited titles, his badge as heir apparent has come to be regarded as his badge as Prince of Wales. Since the reign of Edward III the badge of a feather, or feathers, has been favoured by members of the royal family. The fact that feathers were particularly favoured by Edward, Prince of Wales, 'The Black Prince' has probably helped to give credence to the legend that the feathers badge is that of the Prince of Wales. It was not until Tudor times that the badge assumed its present form and became a badge peculiar to the heir apparent. That the badge is manifestly not that of the Prince of Wales is illustrated by the fact that Edward VI, when heir apparent, used it, and yet he was never Prince of Wales.

I am afraid that not even the heralds are guiltless in perpetrating this error. In 1872 Sir William Withey Gull was granted an honourable augmentation or addition to his coat of arms in recognition of his having attended Edward, Prince of Wales, when he was thought to be dying of typhoid contracted while staying at Lady Londesborough's house in Yorkshire, where the sanitation was not all that it should have been. It was this illness which inspired those famous and awful lines of Alfred Austin, a future Poet Laureate:

> Flash'd from his bed, the electric tidings came,
> He is not better; he is much the same.

The augmentation consisted of a feather, enfiled by a coronet, being added to Sir William's shield of arms on which, understandably, gulls and a serpent (symbol of healing) desported themselves. An admirable idea, but marred by the way in which Sir Albert Woods, Garter King of Arms and Mr Robert Laurie, Clarenceux King of Arms, described the augmentation in the Letters Patent by which it was conferred. The description runs '. . . an Ostrich feather Argent quilled Or enfiled by the Coronet which encircles the Device or Plume of the Prince of Wales . . .'.

The history of the Princes of Wales is, in fact, peppered with solecisms and misconceptions. The creation of the first Prince provides yet another example of this. Edward I had defeated and subdued the Welsh and while progressing through the country in 1284, after slaying the second, and last native Prince of all Wales about eighteen months earlier, his wife Eleanor gave birth to a son at Caernarvon. It is generally thought that Edward made political capital out of this event by showing the infant child to the people of Caernarvon and telling them that here was their Prince. This story has been popularized by historians and more particularly by a Victorian artist

financial backing than was afforded by the revenues of the Earldom of Chester, at least until he became of man's estate. In the event, his father was murdered when he was only fourteen, which may well be why Edward was never created Prince of Wales. Edward came to the throne as Edward III in 1327; he married Philippa of Hainault in 1328 and their first child, Edward, was born on 15 June 1330. This was the famous 'Black Prince' who died a year before his father.

Edward was created Earl of Chester in 1335, Duke of Cornwall (this title did not yet automatically belong to the heir apparent) in 1337 and Prince of Wales on 12 May 1343, just before his thirteenth birthday. When he was created Duke of Cornwall he was the first person to be given that title, which had not previously been used in England, although it was common in France. The dukedom was conferred upon him and the first begotten son of himself and of his heirs being Kings of England and Dukes of Cornwall. Considerable revenues were attached to this title which, under the terms of the Charter, has since been held by the Sovereign's eldest son, either from birth, or from the time of the Sovereign's accession.

The Charter creating Edward Prince of Wales specifies the manner of his investiture. It took place in Parliament at Westminster and, as the Charter was read, so his father performed the actions detailed in it. When the words '*per sertum in capite*' (by a circlet upon his head) were read, so a coronet was placed upon him; at '*et anulum in digito aureum*' a gold ring was placed upon his finger and finally he was invested with a silver rod '*virgam argenteam investivimus*'.

Edward died before ascending the throne and it is interesting to note that his son, Richard, the grandson, but heir apparent to the aged Edward III, although but nine years old was created Prince of Wales and Earl of Chester within six months of his father's death. Thereafter, the Principate of Wales and Earldom of Chester have always been conferred in the same instrument and not as in the case of the Black Prince, separately.

Before a year had passed King Edward had died and Richard had become King. Richard was deposed and murdered in 1399 and the throne was usurped by his cousin, Henry of Bolingbroke. With the consent of Parliament, he created his son Henry, then just twelve years old, Prince of Wales and Earl of Chester, two days after his own coronation. Contemporary ac-

who painted a romantic picture of the King leaning out over the battlements of Caernarvon Castle enacting the scene that I have described. As so often happens, the truth is less glamorous than the legend. In the first place, when Edward was born he was not heir apparent, his elder brother Alfonso being then alive. He did not become heir apparent until some months later when the Court had moved back to England. In the second place, we know that Edward was created Prince of Wales and Earl of Chester on 7 February 1301, in open Parliament at Lincoln, when he was almost seventeen years old.

Whether Edward was invested as Prince of Wales is not known, but it is reasonable to assume that he was, as that would have been customary. He came to the throne as Edward II, in 1307. At that time, he was unmarried, but a month before his coronation, he married Isabelle of France. Nearly four years later, at Windsor Castle, on 13 November 1312, the Queen gave birth to a son, Edward. Within a month, the King had created the infant heir apparent Earl of Chester, but, curiously, never made him Prince of Wales. I suspect that this new title was regarded simply as an appanage, a source of revenue, and that Edward did not consider it necessary to give his son any further

counts do not agree as to the exact form of his investiture, but he was certainly given a golden, rather than a silver rod, a ring and a coronet. He was possibly girded with a belt, as was customary with dukes and earls and was kissed and blessed by his father.

Henry came to the throne in 1413 but died in 1422 leaving a four month old son, Henry VI who was never made Prince of Wales, presumably because his father lacked the opportunity of doing this. However, Henry VI created his own son, Edward, who was said to have been sired by The Holy Ghost, Prince of Wales within a few months of his birth. Edward appears to have been invested while still an infant, which demonstrates the importance attached to investiture in mediaeval England.

Poor Edward was slain at the Battle of Tewkesbury in 1471, less than three weeks before his father died or was murdered in the Tower of London. The victorious Duke of York became Edward IV and his son was at once made Prince of Wales, but was murdered in the Tower after reigning only a few months. His allegedly wicked uncle, Richard III, created his son Edward, Prince of Wales, at a great ceremony in York Cathedral, after which the King, Queen and the young Prince walked in procession through the streets wearing their diadems while the inhabitants 'extolled King Richard above the skies'. Alas, within a year the Queen and her son had both died and Richard had been slain at Bosworth Field.

After Richard's death, Henry Tudor seized the throne and was duly accepted, elected, annointed and crowned as Henry VII. To consolidate his claim dynastically he married, a few months after his coronation, Elizabeth, sister of King Edward IV and coheir of the senior line of Plantagenet. Eight months later the Queen gave birth to a Prince, Arthur. Three years later, in 1489, he was created Prince of Wales and shortly after, the young prince was invested with great solemnity at Westminster. The day before the investiture he was conveyed down the Thames from Sheen in the Royal Barge. As the Barge moved down to Westminster it was joined by the state barges of various dignitaries, including those of the Lord Mayor and the Trade Guilds or Livery Companies of the City of London. It must have been a splendid sight, the fleet of barges gaily bedecked with hangings of rich material, flags and pennons blowing in the breeze and the sound of revelry and minstralsy wafting over the waters of the great river to the crowds merry-making on the banks and, in the centre, the reason for it all, a little boy not four years old. At Whitehall Steps everyone disembarked and went in procession to the Brick Tower, where the King was holding Court. That evening the child Prince was ceremoniously bathed because, in honour of the occasion, he and other nobles were to be made Knights of the Bath on the morrow.

On the following day, the Prince attended Mass and was then led into the royal presence by the Marquess of Berkeley and the Earl of Arundel. He was girded with the Sword, offered the King his Spurs and Shield and then retired, returning to be invested with Mantle, Coronet, Rod and Ring. Thereafter there followed a great banquet.

Poor Arthur died of consumption just after his marriage to Catherine of Aragon, about whom he is said to have remarked 'no woman in the world could be more agreeable'. After his death, his younger brother Henry was accorded both his brother's title of Prince of Wales and his brother's widow as the first of his six wives. I have not lighted on a detailed account of Henry's investiture, other than that he was created Prince of Wales at the Palace of Westminster 'with all solemnite'.

Over a hundred years were to pass before another Prince of Wales was created. It is surprising that Henry VIII, with his strong dynastic urges, never bestowed the Principality on his only legitimate son, Edward, later Edward VI. Every other luxury was lavished on the child except that dignity with which, by now, it had become customary to honour and endow the heir apparent, no matter how tender his years.

The next Prince of Wales, who was invested in great style and in much the same manner as Prince Arthur, was Henry, son of James VI of Scotland who became James I of England on the death of Queen Elizabeth in 1603. He too was escorted on the Thames to Whitehall Steps by the liverymen of London in their barges. It must have been a brave sight, especially as two large creatures, a whale and a dolphin, were towed down the river as part of the pageant. The whale was ridden by a young lady representing Corniea, Queen of Cornwall and the dolphin by Amphion, the genius of Wales, presumably because in classical antiquity Amphion is sometimes regarded as the gentle musician, in contradistinction to his twin Zethus, the rude huntsman.

A few days later the Prince was ceremonially invested. The Court of Requests was transformed into the House of Lords for the occasion and was filled with peers, commoners, ambassadors, the Lord Mayor and Aldermen of London and a great concourse of eminent people. At the appointed time, the Sovereign entered, accompanied by the Earl Marshal, the Lord Chamberlain, the Kings of Arms, Sergeants of Arms and Ushers. The Marquess of Winchester carried the Cap of Maintenance and the Sword of State was borne by Thomas Earl of Arundel. At the beginning of James's reign this nobleman had been restored by Parliament to the honours forfeited by his father, who had died a prisoner in the Tower and who has recently been canonized as St Philip Howard.

When the King was seated upon the throne the Earl Marshal, Lord Chamberlain and the three Kings of Arms went to fetch the Prince. The Prince's procession entered, led by the Earl Marshal and the Lord Chamberlain and the two junior Kings of Arms. Then came the twenty-five Knights of the Bath who had been dubbed in honour of the occasion, wearing robes of purple satin. These were followed by the insignia bearers led by Garter King of Arms carrying the Letters Patent creating Henry Prince of Wales and Earl of Chester. The Earl of Sussex carried the Mantle of purple velvet, the Earl of Huntingdon bearing the train; the Earl of Cumberland carried the Sword; the Earl of Rutland the Ring, the Earl of Derby the Rod or Virge of Gold and the Earl of Shrewsbury the Cap and Circlet. The Prince habited in a velvet surcoat, was supported by the Earls of Northampton (the Lord Privy Seal) and Nottingham (the Lord Admiral).

The procession advanced towards the throne, stopping three times and bowing to the King. On arriving at the throne, the Prince knelt before his father, Garter kissed the Patent and handed it to the Lord Chamberlain, who handed it to the King, who accepted it and passed it to the Earl of Salisbury, who read it. As the words of investiture contained in the Patent were read, so the actions were performed. The King handed the Mantle to the Prince's assistants, who placed it upon him; he was then girded with the Sword, had the Cap and Circlet or Coronet put upon his head and was then invested with the Ring and golden Rod.

The Prince then kissed his father's hand and in return was embraced by him upon his cheek. Two noblemen then conducted the Prince to his seat in Parliament, to the left of the Throne, where he sat while the Deputy for the Clerk of the Crown, kneeling, read out the names of those who had witnessed the Charter of creation. This done the King and Prince withdrew in a great and solemn procession.

Later the Prince dined in state with the new Knights of the Bath, the King dining privately. The next two days were given over to a variety of entertainments. There was a 'most rich and Royall maske of ladies', a joust at the Tiltyard, re-enactments of naval triumphs and a great display of fireworks. 'Time hath its revolutions' for less than two and a half years after these rejoicings Henry was dead and his place as heir apparent and Duke of Cornwall and Rothesay had fallen to his younger brother Charles, later to become 'King Charles the Martyr'.

Charles was not created and invested Prince of Wales until four years after his brother's tragic death. From all accounts, the manner of his investiture was in all respects similar to Henry's, except that perhaps the rejoicings were a little muted, although one account states that 'pleasant Trophies and ingenious devices met him upon the water than ever was at any former creation of any Prince of Wales'. This was the last time a Prince of Wales was invested until 1911.

It will be seen from the description I have given, that there are many similarities between the formal investiture of a prince, the introduction of a peer into the House of Lords and the coronation of a monarch: the three bows; the delivery and reading of the Patent; the investing with ornaments; the placing in Parliament; the kiss; the wearing of robes; the presence of the great officers with Sword of State and Cap of Maintenance; the formal banquet – elements with which we have now become familiar. This is important because the investiture ceremony in 1911 was a kind of amalgam of old rites and traditions, transformed to a certain extent to meet the political exigencies of the twentieth century.

But before considering the 1911 investiture I must explain what happened during the three centuries when there were no investitures.

James I died in 1625, being succeeded by his son Charles I. Charles married Henrietta Maria of France in the same year and in 1630 their second, but first surviving child was born, Charles, Duke of Cornwall and Rothesay, later to become Charles II. There is no evidence that this Prince was ever created Prince of Wales. He is sometimes referred to as such, but in the absence of any Charter or Patent of creation, I am firmly of the opinion that, whatever may have been his father's intentions, he never carried them out. The same is true of James II's son, James Francis Edward, known to history as 'The Old Pretender'. He was born two months before his father left the country and so was held to have abdicated. Like his uncle Charles he was referred to by contemporaries as Prince of Wales, but there is no evidence that the title was formally bestowed upon him.

The next Prince of Wales was George Augustus, son of King George I. His father succeeded in 1714 under the terms of the Act of Settlement, being the nearest Protestant heir. He created his son Prince of Wales three weeks before his coronation, but dispensed with the ceremony of investiture. The Patent simply declared that George was confirmed and invested. This set a pattern for future creations. The next Princes of Wales were Frederick Lewis, son of George II, but who predeceased his father; George, grandson of George II and later George III; his son George, who became Prince Regent and then George IV; next was Edward, eldest son of Queen Victoria, who became Prince of Wales when one month old and, lastly, George, later George V, who was created Prince of Wales before his father was crowned as Edward VII.

When George V succeeded his father he followed precedent and within two months of his accession created his son Edward Albert Christian George Andrew Patrick David (known to his family as David, and to history as Edward VIII and the Duke of Windsor), Prince of Wales.

That the old custom of investiture, which for princes, peers and even heralds had not been performed for so many generations, should be revived for Prince Edward was due to the imagination of Mr David (later Earl) Lloyd-George, Chancellor of the Exchequer in Mr Herbert Asquith's Government. It was not, however, part of his plan that the investiture should be what it had always been before, a parliamentary occasion staged at Westminster supported by the considerable pomp and wealth of the City of London. If it were going to happen, it was to be in Wales. The only question was where – at Cardiff, the principal City in Wales, at Chester, because of the Prince's title of Earl of Chester, or at Caernarvon, where the first English Prince was born.

A committee was formed under the Chairmanship of the Earl of Plymouth, which may seem a strange choice but the distinguished Earl was, among other things, Lord Lieutenant of the County of Glamorgan. In the end the Committee, I suspect not uninfluenced by Mr Lloyd-George, who had been made Constable of Caernarvon Castle in 1908, recommended Caernarvon. With this recommendation the King concurred. As the King remarked in his speech at the investiture, Caernarvon appealed not only to the imagination of the Welsh people, but to that of the whole Empire, 'carrying the mind back more than 600 years to the time when the first Edward sought to establish peace among the mountains of Wales by associating the title and honours of the Prince of Wales with the heir to the Crown of England'.

Once the venue had been chosen preparations for the ceremony were swiftly put in hand. The Earl Marshal and the Officers of Arms were responsible for the actual ceremony of investiture. The Office of Works, under Sir Schomberg McDonnell, undertook the preparation of the Castle and the provision of stands and seats. The Lord Chamberlain made all the arrangements for the Royal Family and the police, military and other departments looked after those areas which naturally came under their authority.

The first and most important matter to be considered and settled was the form which the investiture should take. Clearly it would have to be more interesting than that which took place in Parliament and cannot have taken above a quarter of an hour to perform. Clearly, also, there could be no placing of the Prince in his seat in Parliament. The ancient form of investiture would obviously have to be observed, or the whole ceremony would deteriorate into an empty pageant rather than a constitutional act. The question was how the ceremony could be augmented so as to inflate its significance both with regard to the sentiments of the Welsh people and to the vast number of important guests who would be summoned to Caernarvon to witness it. I suspect that the planners drew heavily on the ceremony of the coronation in working out a suitable ceremonial.

For the procession and investiture there were

ELIZABETH THE SECOND BY THE GRACE OF GOD OF THE UNITED KINGDOM OF GREAT BRITAIN AND NORTHERN IRELAND AND OF OUR OTHER REALMS AND TERRITORIES QUEEN HEAD OF THE COMMONWEALTH DEFENDER OF THE FAITH To all Lords Spiritual and Temporal and all other Our Subjects whatsoever to whom these Presents shall come Greeting Know Ye that We have made and created and by these Our Letters Do make and create Our most dear Son Charles Philip Arthur George Prince of the United Kingdom of Great Britain and Northern Ireland Duke of Cornwall and Rothesay Earl of Carrick Baron of Renfrew Lord of the Isles and Great Steward of Scotland PRINCE OF WALES and EARL OF CHESTER And to the same Our most dear Son Charles Philip Arthur George Have given and granted and by this Our present Charter Do give grant and confirm the name style title dignity and honour of the same Principality and Earldom And him Our most dear Son Charles Philip Arthur George as has been accustomed We do ennoble and invest with the said Principality and Earldom by girting him with a Sword by putting a Coronet on his head and a Gold Ring on his finger and also by delivering a Gold Rod into his hand that he may preside there and may direct and defend those parts To hold to him and his heirs Kings of the United Kingdom of Great Britain and Northern Ireland and of Our other Realms and Territories Heads of the Commonwealth for ever Wherefore We Will and strictly command for Us Our heirs and successors that Our most dear Son Charles Philip Arthur George may have the name style title state dignity and honour of the Principality of Wales and Earldom of Chester aforesaid unto him and his heirs Kings of the United Kingdom of Great Britain and Northern Ireland and of Our other Realms and Territories Heads of the Commonwealth as is above mentioned In Witness whereof We have caused these Our Letters to be made Patent Witness Ourself at Westminster the twenty - sixth day of July in the seventh year of Our Reign.

By Warrant under The Queen's Sign Manual

COLDSTREAM

Letters Patent creating Prince Charles, the Queen's eldest son, Prince of Wales and Earl of Chester on 16 July 1958.

precedents and also for the kiss, which was made more significant by it following an act of homage, similar to that used at a coronation. The coronation takes place within the Communion Service and, the Welsh being a God-fearing people, it was considered appropriate to include a religious service after the actual investiture. Then, just as a sovereign is presented to those in Westminster Abbey for election before the coronation ceremony, so it was decided to present the Prince to the people, not for election, but for acclamation and in imitation of what Edward I is thought to have done centuries earlier, at the end of the ceremony. In this way, a new ceremony encompassing an ancient ritual was born and was, in substance, repeated on 1 July 1969, when the present Prince of Wales was invested at Caernarvon.

When the Queen created Prince Charles Prince of Wales and Earl of Chester on 26 July 1958, shortly before his tenth birthday, she promised that she would publicly invest him when he was older. In 1967 she asked the Earl Marshal, the late Bernard, Duke of Norfolk, who had masterminded two coronations

and Sir Winston Churchill's funeral if he would be responsible for the whole ceremony of investiture. A little reluctantly, or so he said, he agreed. Of course, a powerful committee was set up but it was essentially the Earl Marshal who held all the strings in his hands, who advised the Sovereign and master-minded the whole operation. Garter King of Arms, who was then Sir Anthony Wagner, was his principal Staff Officer and Mr Rodney Dennys, Somerset Herald, and myself were appointed to assist him, so I found myself intimately concerned with the ceremony from the beginning.

Rather than give detailed accounts of the 1911 and 1969 ceremonies, I shall simply touch on certain salient points, comparing the two occasions and relying on newspaper reports and personal accounts for details of the earlier ceremony and on my own notes and reminiscences for those of the last investiture.

There is no doubt that we drew heavily on the 1911 ceremony when planning Prince Charles' investiture. Precedents had been set and clearly we were expected to follow them. Obviously, it would be wrong to plan a state ceremony simply for the benefit of the media, but equally the media cannot be ignored. Even in 1911 arrangements were made for 300 representatives of the press, 30 photographers and as many 'cinematographists', as they were called, to be accommodated.

In 1969 we were faced with a huge demand from the world press and particularly from television companies. Whether we wanted it or not, we were putting on a show which hundreds of millions would watch live, and countless others would see in replays. What happened at Caernarvon would become a permanent historical record; it was a sobering thought. Basically, we met this new challenge by opening up both the ceremony and the venue. The heavy green and white striped canopy over the dais, which partially obscured the actual ceremony of investiture in 1911 gave way to Lord Snowdon's imaginative, lofty, transparent canopy, which could be penetrated by the eyes of the cameras. The awnings which shielded the 1911 crowds from the rain (or, as it turned out, from the intense sun) were abandoned. When asked what would happen if it rained, the Earl Marshal gave a typically laconic reply, 'You'll get wet'. In 1911 there were just two processions – the Prince's and the King's. We added a series of small or, in some cases, not so small processions which entered the castle at five minute intervals so as to sustain the interest of those within the castle and of those viewing the proceedings on television.

The castle is a long, sausage-shaped building about 600 feet long and 200 feet wide. It runs East and West and consists of a high wall punctuated at intervals by nine towers. At the West end, down by the water, is the Eagle Tower and Water Gate where the first Prince is said to have been born and it is through this tower that all the processions entered. They then proceeded down the Inner Bailey, up a few steps into the Outer Bailey towards the end of which the royal dais was erected. In 1911, those processing sat on either side of the Throne, the choir of over 400 being ranged behind it. We placed the choir to the North of the dais and sat those in the processions behind, or in the case of very important people, on little gilt chairs, which the Earl Marshal called his 'flower-pots', on the grass near the dais. In the centre of the North wall of the castle just at the end of the Outer Bailey, is the King's Gate, which leads into the town and through this gate the public were admitted. Opposite is the Chamberlain Tower, which was used on both occasions as the Prince's retiring room. On either side of the wide central pathway running the length of the castle stands were erected for guests. Here again there was less crowding, for reasons of comfort and

security, than in 1911. In that year over 7500 persons were admitted, which was over 3000 more than in 1969. As at a coronation, the guests were divided into categories ranging from the *Corps Diplomatique*, to representatives of education, the Trades Unions, the Arts, Sport, Local Authorities and 200 school children.

On both occasions, guests had to arrive in the morning, the only difference being that in 1969 all handbags had to be searched as there was a constant security threat from minority Welsh Nationalist elements, a threat which greatly added to our difficulties and would have caste a blight over the ceremony had not the loyalty and enthusiasm of the great majority overshadowed the protests of the eccentric fringe.

Prince Edward, at his investiture arrived at the Water Gate, having first received and responded to a loyal address. Here he had his first opportunity of utilizing the few Welsh phrases which Mr Lloyd-George had carefully taught him. In the Eagle Tower he was joined by druids, Officers of Arms, the mayors of 29 Welsh boroughs, the Mayor of Chester and his suite, Welsh Members of Parliament and members of his household. Supported by Lords Plymouth and Kenyon his procession made its way to the Chamberlain Tower, those not taking part in the actual ceremony going to their places. A little later the King and Queen arrived. Preceded by Officers of Arms, sheriffs and lieutenants of Welsh Counties and Peers of the Realm in their parliament robes, they moved towards the dais in procession.

What we did in 1969 was to extricate various groups of people from these two processions and form them into separate processions. These processions were marshalled at the Shire Hall, just near the King's Gate. They then moved, at the times appointed, along the outside of the North wall of the castle and round to the Eagle Tower. In this way, those in the stands which had been erected in the moat were able to see as much of the processions as those inside the castle.

The Officers of Arms were the first to leave the Shire Hall, but we got no further than the Eagle Tower, as we had duties to perform. We were followed by a long procession of representatives of Welsh youth, but they did not walk up through the castle either; they stood on a plot of grass just inside the Eagle Tower to await the Prince's arrival. The next two processions, those who would take part in the Prince's procession and the Councillors and Mayor of Caernarvon and his suite, also waited in the Eagle Tower. There then followed a series of processions, all of which moved down the whole length of the castle to their places at the East end. First came the

Officers and Members of the Gorsedd of Bards and of the National Eisteddfod Court, clad in what to philistine English eyes looked like nightgowns, but very colourful nonetheless. The Mayor of Chester, followed by the Mayors of the Boroughs, County Boroughs and Capital City of Cardiff, accompanied by their Clerks, and Mace Bearers formed the next procession, splendid in their civic robes and chains of office. After them came the Chairmen of the County Councils of Wales, the Queen's High Sheriffs of the Welsh Counties, most Members of Parliament for the Welsh constituencies (I think there was but one conscientious objector), Peers of Parliament nominated by the Lord Chancellor and, finally, representatives of the churches in Wales.

Immediately after the last procession had moved down the castle the Queen's bodyguards took up their posts, the Gentlemen at Arms in the Upper Bailey (we called it Ward in 1969) and the Yeoman of the Guard in the Lower. Then came the junior members of the Royal Family, who were received by the Mayor of Caernarvon as Deputy Constable of the castle, the Earl of Snowdon as Constable and Mr John Silkin, the then Minister of Public Buildings and Works.

At 2.35 p.m. the Prince of Wales arrived in his carriage accompanied by a Prince of Wales' Escort of the Household Cavalry. He was received in the same manner as the junior royals, but, as he entered the Eagle Tower his personal banner for use in Wales was broken over the tower. We regarded the use of the word banner in the Ceremonial as a definite victory as it was the first time in a Royal Ceremonial that a banner had been called a banner rather than a standard. As I have indicated elsewhere a standard is a long tapering flag and has nothing to do with the rectangular flag broken at Caernarvon. This banner

Edward, Prince of Wales with Queen Mary after his Investiture at Caernarvon Castle in 1911.

Opposite: The Queen in her robes as Sovereign of the Order of the Bath at an installation ceremony at Westminster Abbey in 1975.

was an innovation, consisting of the old coat of arms of Llewelyn, Prince of Gwyneth and last native Prince of Wales, with a green shield in the centre on which is a representation of the coronet of the Prince of Wales. In 1911 the banner broken was of the Prince's actual coat of arms as Prince of Wales.

The Prince's procession to the Chamberlain Tower was composed of eight Welsh dignitaries such as the Presidents of the National Museum of Wales, the National Library of Wales and of the National Eisteddfod Court. Sir Hugo Boothby bore the Banner of the Red Dragon, the Prince's badge and Sir Watkin Williams-Wynn that of Prince Llewelyn. Next came the Secretary of State for Wales, the Rt Honourable Mr George Thomas (now Speaker of the House of Commons), the peers who would bear the princely insignia, two heralds and the Prince between his supporting peers, Lords Dynevor and Davies. The representatives of Welsh youth fell in behind the procession. The Prince, the Secretary of State, the insignia bearers, the heralds and his supporting peers entered the Chamberlain Tower, while the rest went to their places at the eastern end of the castle.

In 1911 the insignia bearers had been in the Royal Procession and had had to go and collect the Prince at a signal given by the Earl Marshal. At the investiture of Prince Charles, the Prince's procession was already in the Chamberlain Tower and was brought to the dais by Garter King of Arms, when signalled to do so by the Earl Marshal.

After the Prince's procession, the Royal Party arrived. The Queen, the Duke of Edinburgh and Princess Anne in the first carriage, the Queen Mother, Princess Margaret and the Master of the Horse in the second, and members of the household in the third.

On arrival at the Water Gate the Equerry in Waiting knocked on the door and demanded admission in the name of the Queen. The door was opened and Lord Snowdon appeared, in a curious sort of page-boy uniform of his own design, with a vast key on a velvet cushion. 'Madam', he said, 'I surrender the key of this castle into your Majesty's hand'. The Queen touched the key and replied: 'Sir Constable, I return the key of this castle into your keeping'. The Queen then entered the Eagle Tower and, as she did so, the Prince of Wales' Banner was struck and the Royal Banner broken over the Tower.

The Queen Mother and the two Princesses moved towards the dais, being followed five minutes later by the Royal Procession, led by the Mayor of Caernarvon. This was not a long procession, being

Opposite: The Queen and the Duke of Edinburgh arriving at St Paul's for the Silver Jubilee Thanksgiving Service.

formed on much the same lines as that at the Opening of Parliament, but with the Lords Lieutenant of the Welsh Counties being included.

I will not describe the actual investiture since it followed traditional lines. In 1911 the Home Secretary, Mr (later Sir) Winston Churchill read the Letters Patent. In 1969 Mr James Callaghan did likewise but a Welsh translation was also read by Mr George Thomas. On both occasions a loyal address was read and responded to by the Prince but in 1969 both speeches were in Welsh and I am told that the Prince's accent was quite remarkably good.

The religious service was similar on both occasions, as were the Presentations. Three Officers of Arms, the Earl Marshal, the Lord Great Chamberlain and Lord Anglesey (in 1911 it had been Lord Beauchamp) carrying the Sword of State led the Prince and his parents to a balcony constructed above Queen

The Queen placing the coronet on the head of her son, Charles Prince of Wales, at his Investiture in 1969.

Opposite: *The Queen with the Prince of Wales at one of the presentations to the people following his formal investiture at Caernarvon Castle.*

Eleanor's Gate at the eastern end of the castle. Here the Queen presented the Prince to the people assembled below; this was repeated at the King's gate and at the top of the steps dividing the two Wards or Bailies. Each Presentation was heralded by really magnificent fanfares, sounded by trumpeters placed in strategic positions on the battlements.

A great procession was now formed to lead the royal party to the Eagle Tower and thence back through the town to the assembly point, which was the premises of Ferodo Limited. In 1911 it had been Griffith's Crossing, a Railway crossing just outside the town, but on this occasion it seemed wiser for reasons of security as well as being more practical, to accept Ferodo's offer to lend their premises.

The secret of success in a great ceremony like the investiture, where 413 people took part in the processions, many of whom had never processed before, is to keep most of them in ignorance. Tell them nothing except to do what they are told. Then it is up to the trained and carefully briefed marshals to move them along at the right speed and eventually hand them over to other ushers, who will put them in their correct positions. To this end the marshals must be seen to have authority, which is why we chose them from people used to exercising authority, put them into uniform and issued them with batons and told them to get on with the job.

I have mentioned uniforms, so let me conclude this account with a brief sartorial note. When we first asked the Earl Marshal about the dress regulations he wanted promulgated, I remember him saying something like 'We want lots of colour, lots to interest people, let them wear uniforms, robes, all their glad rags. At heart everyone likes dressing up and people like to see others dressed up'. And so it was. Even the regulations for guests permitted almost anything to be worn '. . . Service or Civilian Uniform . . . Robes of Office or Academic Dress, or Morning Dress, with which Stars of Orders, Neck and other Decorations and Medals may also be worn . . . with Dark Lounge Suits only Medals may be worn . . .'.

Prince Edward had complained about the 'fantastic costume designed for the occasion, consisting of white satin breeches and a mantle and surcoat of purple velvet edged with ermine'. This was not inflicted on Prince Charles. He wore Naval uniform with both the Collar and Riband of the Garter, which is unusual. Naturally, both Princes had to be invested with the robe, as this was traditional. The rod, ring and sword had been made for the 1911 ceremony to the design of Mr Goscombe John, R.A. The circlet with which Prince Edward was invested, a little pantomime coronet, was incorrect as it had no arch. Prince Charles turned down the idea of using this ridiculous coronet, so we had to look for another. We knew that the Duke of Windsor had the coronet he wore at his father's coronation, in his house in France. We also knew that this conformed to the regulations laid down by a Royal Warrant of Charles II in 1661, the coronet being the same as St Edward's Crown, except that it had but a single arch. The question was whether it would be politic to ask if we might borrow it. Eventually, it was decided to have a new coronet made. The Goldsmiths' Company of London was permitted to present the coronet and Mr Louis Osman was commissioned to design and make it, but it was made clear that the design must conform to the regulations inasmuch as the coronet must have one arch supporting an orb and about the rim there had to be fleurs-de-lis alternating with crosses formy.

The Queen and the Prince of Wales approved the design in January 1969. In April the copper mock-up was ready, but it differed in several details from the original design. However, it was too late to alter it and the coronet was made, not in the traditional way, but by 'growing' it in a specially prepared electroplating bath for nearly three days.

What emerged was a 24 carat gold coronet weighing 105 ounces; this was set with gems and, happily for the Goldsmiths' Company, exempted from purchase tax. A person with half-closed eyes and a charitable disposition might say that the coronet conformed to King Charles' rules, although only just. It was not a traditional design and opinion was divided as to whether Mr Osman had succeeded.

Chapter 7

The Orders of Chivalry

The modern conception of knighthood, indeed, the modern knight, would hardly be recognized in mediaeval England. Today a man is knighted by the Sovereign as a reward for services rendered. The Queen, or her representative, dubs him, that is taps him on the shoulder with a sword, and he becomes a knight. Until quite recently a new knight could not call himself 'Sir' until the ceremony of dubbing had been performed but now he may do so just as soon as the conferment of the honour is announced.

No longer is knighthood concerned with military prowess, the code of chivalry or tenure of land. Non-christians, men who have never fought for their country and in some recent honours lists, men who in the Middle Ages would have been called 'notorious sinners' receive the accolade. The coinage has become sadly debased. However, this is not a phenomenon of the twentieth century, the erosion of the high ideals of the twelfth century has been going on for a very long time.

Knighthood and chivalry are almost synonymous. Knighthood was originally a system of feudal tenure by which a knight held his lands from his lord in return for service. This service was both military and personal. A knight had to equip himself with a horse and armour and be prepared to attend his overlord in the field for forty days each year, he also had to assist his lord with the administration of justice and with the ceremonies of his court. But this was not all, the tenant knight was further burdened with financial obligations, such as helping to ransom his lord if this were necessary and providing a dower for his lord's eldest daughter when she married. There were many other tiresome and expensive obligations, but the one which caused more resentment than most was the custom that when a tenant died leaving an heir under twenty-one years of age or an heiress under sixteen,

the child became the ward of his lord, who then took all the profits of the child's lands and could dispose of him, or her in marriage.

It would be reasonable to suppose that when the system of warfare altered and a national army replaced the feudal host that the feudal system itself would change. The trouble was that it was so profitable to the Crown and greater nobility that it was retained and although service was not required, all the financial obligations remained. Feudalism was not finally laid to rest until the end of the seventeenth century.

Knighthood was not simply a form of feudal tenure and a means of keeping equipped knights-at-arms ready to fight offensive or defensive battles at a moment's notice, it was a personal dignity and an honourable degree which carried with it obligations of a very different sort from those practical ones, some of which I have detailed. A knight was expected to honour the code of chivalry, or knightly conduct. This has been summed up by Leon Gautier in his 'Ten Commandments' of chivalric behaviour.

A knight must believe in and be obedient to the teachings of the Church, which he must be willing to defend; he must pity and defend the weak and champion right and good against the forces of evil; he must love his country and be merciless to the infidel; he must obey his lord in all such things as are not contrary to his duty to God; he must be loyal to truth and to his pledged word and he must give generously. One has only to read of the violence, greed and lust of the Middle Ages to realize that this code was often 'more honour'd in the breach than the observance' but it was an ideal and many tried to live up to it.

The road to knighthood was for a boy of noble blood first to serve as a page in a great household, learning how to use weapons and learning the system of courtly and chivalrous behaviour. The next step was for him to be made a squire to a knight or noble by being given silver spurs. This meant acting as his master's valet and close personal attendant in both peace and war, with a view to receiving the honour of knighthood when he was about twenty. This was conferred ceremoniously and it is perhaps worth looking at a particular and, at one time, quite common ceremony of knighting, which has some relevance today.

The squire who was to be knighted was attended by two other squires. On the eve of the ceremony, under their direction, he was shaved and had his hair cut. They then led him to a bath hung within and without with linen and rich cloths; they undressed him and when he was in the bath two 'ancient and grave knights' attended him 'to inform, instruct and counsel him touching the order and feats of chivalry'. This done the squires put the candidate into a plain bed until he was dry. They then dressed him in a white shirt and russet habit, like a hermit's and led him to partake of a collation, after which he, together with a priest and his squires, kept vigil in the chapel, 'bestowing himself in orisons and prayers' until daybreak.

At sunrise he made his confession and attended Matins and Mass. After this he went to bed, but not before offering a candle for the Church and a coin for the person who would knight him.

Later the candidate was aroused, dressed and taken before the king, if the king were conferring the knighthood. His future squire would hold his sheathed sword by the tip, his golden spurs hanging from the hilt. These were presented to the king who gave the right spur to the 'most noble and gentle' knight present, who fixed it to the candidate's right heel, making the sign of the Cross on his knee. Another knight did likewise with the left spur. The king then girded him with his sword, embraced him, lifted his right hand and smote him on the neck or shoulder saying 'be thou a good knight'. This done, the new knight went to the chapel where he swore, with his right hand on the altar, to defend the Church. He then took off his sword and offered it on the altar. As he came out the king's master cook said: 'If you do anything contrary to the order of chivalry (which God forbid) I shall hack the spurs from your heels'. He then claimed the spurs as his fee.

From this account, it will be seen that knighthood was not just military, nor principally concerned with tenure, but had an almost sacramental and essentially Christian aspect.

That the new knight took a bath on the eve of his creation has led some to think that the Order of the Bath was instituted by Henry IV when a batch of new knights was created more or less in the manner described above, in honour of his coronation. However, the taking of a bath was an ancient ceremony which Henry revived and it later became customary for kings to create a number of knights in this ceremonious manner on occasions such as their coronations, or on the creation of their sons as Princes of Wales. These knights came to be called Knights of the Bath, but this was not an order of knighthood with statutes and a chapel like the Order of the Garter. Really, they were unattached knights, or knights bachelor but, because of the manner of their creation, they were given a special name and social, but not constitutional pre-eminence.

After the coronation of Charles II the tradition of making Knights of the Bath lapsed until the so-called Order was revived, but really instituted in 1725 by George I as a capitular Order with a corporate identity.

The idea of creating special Orders of fraternities of knights, in addition to ordinary knights, goes back to the time of the Crusades.

Whatever one's view of the Crusades, or Wars of the Cross, which aimed to rid the Holy Land of the Saracens, they had the effect of bringing together the flower of chivalry from all over Europe, united in a common and basically unselfish purpose. Instead of fighting each other, they fought a common enemy, the enemy which every true knight was bound to fight, the Infidel. Out of the Crusades were born the monastic orders of knighthood. At first these were no more than groups of knights who united to protect and care for pilgrims to the Holy Land and to guard the Holy Sepulchre. Soon they were officially recognized and exerted a powerful influence in Christendom.

The first of these Orders was known as the Hospitallers or Knights Hospitallers. Founded by a Benedictine monk, the Blessed Gerard, the Order built a hospital near the Holy Sepulchre, capable of accommodating two thousand sick pilgrims, and soon assumed a military character as it needed to defend its property as well as those for whom it cared. As early as 1113, only forty-seven years after the Norman conquest of Britain, Pope Paschal II approved the Order and his approval was solemnly confirmed by a Bull of Pope Calixtus II six years later. The Order was dedicated to St John the Baptist and so became known as the Hospitaller Order of St John of Jerusalem. The head of the Order was the Grand Master also, and more humbly, called the Servant of the Poor in Jesus Christ. There were three degrees in the Order: knights who took vows of poverty, chastity and obedience; ecclesiastics who were chaplains, and

H.R.H. Prince Arthur, Duke of Connaught, Grand Prior of the Order of St John, outside St John's Gate, Clerkenwell, at a Ceremony of the Order in 1920.

subalterns who roughly corresponded to squires.

When the old Kingdom of Jerusalem fell to the Infidel in 1306 the knights established themselves in Rhodes, which they held until it was captured by Soliman the Magnificent in 1522. Eight years later, the Holy Roman Emperor, Charles V, granted the Order the Island of Malta, which it ruled until Napoleon Bonaparte took possession of the island in 1798. Later, in 1815, the Congress of Vienna allotted Malta to the British. The Order re-established itself in Naples and afterwards in Rome, where it exists to this day, being now a charitable organization with priories and associations throughout the world. Although the Order has undergone many vicissitudes and changes in its long history, it is still an international Order of noble and eminent men. It is exclusively Roman Catholic and is devoted to the care of the poor and·sick. It has been known by many names, but its official style today is The Sovereign Military Order of St John of Jerusalem of Rhodes and of Malta, but it is more usually called The Order of Malta.

The Knights Templar was a similar Order, but when it could no longer fulfil its original purpose of protecting pilgrims, it was not kept busy ruling an island as was the Order of St John, but indulged in such worldly activities as lending money at high rates of interest. For this and other reasons it was abolished by Pope Clement V by the Bull *Considerates Dudum* in 1312 and the property it held was in most countries transferred to the Hospitallers.

The Teutonic Knights of the Virgin Mary was an Order founded in 1190 and was essentially Germanic. It virtually died in 1410 after the battle of Tannenberg, but it still exists as a religious Order in Germany.

The Hospitallers founded a priory in England in 1154 and the Prior, who later was regularly summoned to sit in the House of Lords, lived at Clerkenwell in London. The Order acquired much property in England which, of course, was augmented by receiving the Templars' possessions in 1312. One has only to consider how many streets in England are called St John Street, to appreciate the landed wealth of the Order, for, in most cases, the Order owned property in these areas.

Henry VIII suppressed the Order, along with the monastic orders, although the last Grand Prior, Sir Thomas Tresham, was never debarred from sitting in the House of Lords. Just over a hundred years ago, an Association of the Order was re-established in Britain and this now thrives, being composed of more knights than were in the mediaeval Grand Priory, but having none of the power which stems from the possession of wealth and property.

At the beginning of the last century, a number of gentlemen sought to re-establish the order in England, but not as a Roman Catholic Order. Their intentions were good and in May 1888, Queen Victoria granted their Association a Royal Charter. The Crown assumed the Sovereignty of the new Order, which now consists of a Grand Prior (the Duke of Gloucester), a Lord Prior (Lord Caccia), various Great Officers and six other grades, Bailiffs, or Dames Grand Cross, Knights and Dames, Chaplains and Commanders, Officers, Serving Brothers and Sisters and Esquires. The official designation of the Order is 'The Grand Priory of the Most Venerable Order of the Hospital of St John of Jerusalem', but, for brevity, it may be styled 'The Order of St John'. The insignia of the Order is worn before campaign medals, but after other Orders. However, membership confers neither title nor precedence.

Admission to the various grades of the Order is solemnly conferred at a ceremony of investiture, which is similar to that at which the Queen distributes decorations. This ceremony can be performed by the Queen as Sovereign Head of the Order, but is usually presided over by the Grand Prior or the Lord Prior. When I was made a Knight of Justice of the Order, I was tapped on the shoulder by the Duke of Gloucester in St James's Palace, had the cross hung round my neck and a black cloak, emblazoned with the badge of the Order, placed over my shoulders. It was all over in a few seconds, but I was glad that the ceremony was still performed as it lent significance and a sense of occasion to the award.

The real *raison d'être* of the Order is to maintain and develop the St John Ambulance and also the Opthalmic Hospital in Jerusalem. It is essentially a charitable body, maintaining an ancient ideal and, by a stroke of good fortune, having its headquarters in the old pre-Reformation Grand Priory at Clerkenwell.

The ancient Christian and ceremonial tradition is maintained by holding an annual commemoration service in St Paul's Cathedral. This is a great occasion. First the Members of Chapter-General, the Governing Body of the Order, proceed in their robes down the nave. They are followed by representatives of the priories and commanderies of the Order in the Commonwealth. Finally, to the sound of trumpets, the Great Officers of the Order and the Bailiffs followed by their Esquires bearing banners of their personal arms lead in the Sheriffs and Lord Mayor of London, robed and attended by the Serjeant-at-Arms

Three views of the buildings of the Priory of the Order of St John from a seventeenth century engraving by Hollar.

and the Sword Bearer. A hymn is sung, the Cross, Sword, Standard of the Order and the Colour of St John Ambulance are received at the high altar and the service continues, ending with a processional withdrawal, again to a fanfare of trumpets.

It must have been the existence of these early monastic Orders of Knighthood that suggested to later Christian kings the idea of founding lay Orders of knights. In early feudal days such Orders would have served no particular purpose, but when it became more and more usual for people who did not want to perform their military service to commute it by paying a fine called 'scutage', the Sovereign looked for a group of knights who would be particularly bound to him in a manner more chivalrous than feudal and who would enhance his prestige and power. These thoughts may have passed through the mind of Edward III when he founded the Most Noble Order of the Garter in 1348, although it is well known that he was also devoted to the romantic idea of chivalry as exemplified by the legend of King Arthur and his Knights of the Round Table.

The oft-told story of why the Order was called 'The Garter', or 'The Blue Garter' is that, while dancing at Calais, a lady, possibly the Countess of Salisbury, 'The Fair Maid of Kent', lost a garter. King Edward retrieved it and tied it round his own leg to the amusement of the courtiers. The King rebuked them by saying '*Honi soit qui mal y pense*' – 'Evil be to him who thinks badly of it', or 'Evil be to him who evil thinks', which is the motto of the Order.

Dr Margaret Murray has improved on this legend by suggesting that the fact that the Countess wore a Garter was a sign that she was a witch, a member of the Old Religion and that Edward picked it up with alacrity and tied it round his leg because he, too, was a believer, a sort of Masonic handshake. If this were true, his rebuke to the courtiers would have made more sense, for who would have been shocked by his action if it were not more than an act of gallantry? The only trouble is that the garter was the wrong colour to have esoteric significance, it should have been red, not blue. On the other hand, there were twenty-six original knights, the King and Prince of Wales being included, which is two covens of witches . . .

Whatever the origin of the Order it is the oldest and most sought-after. Like the old religious orders, it was an Order of christian chivalry and was assigned a heavenly patron and protector in the person of St George.

An illustration from Bruges' Garter Book *(c. 1430), made for William Bruges, first Garter King of Arms. It shows Edward III, the founder of the Order.*

The Roman Catholic Church has recently demoted St George, but although the stories of his life may be legendary, he would seem to have been an early christian martyr, whose cult and fame, whether or not it were based on fact or myth, had spread to England before the Norman Conquest. In 1222 his Feast Day was included among the lesser holidays in England and it must be supposed that Edward was acquainted with the Acts of St George, in which he is portrayed as a military hero and paragon of chivalry, and for this reason selected him as a typically noble and romantic saint to watch over the fortunes of his new Order.

The Chapel of the Order is St George's Chapel, Windsor, and every year, on the Monday before the Royal Ascot Race Meeting, a Service is held there and, if there are any new knights, these are invested and installed on this day.

The investiture of a new knight takes place in the Throne Room at Windsor Castle. The Knights and Officers of the Order, that is the Prelate, the Chancellor, the Register, the Secretary, Garter King of Arms and the Gentleman Usher of the Black Rod, take their places. The Sovereign enters, accompanied by the Duke of Edinburgh and usually also by the

Prince of Wales and the Queen Mother. Garter and Black Rod conduct them to their places and then stand on either side of the Sovereign.

The Lord's Prayer is recited and Garter and Black Rod collect the two knights who will support the knight elect, and then leave the Throne Room to summon him. When they have returned and gone to their places the Sovereign says 'My Lords and Ladies, pray be seated'. The Chancellor calls the name of the knight elect, who is conducted before the Sovereign by his two supporters.

Garter hands the velvet garter, embroidered with the motto of the Order to the Sovereign, who, helped by the supporting peers, buckles it on the knight elect's left leg. In fact, either one of the supporters, or Garter, kneels down and symbolically environs, with a gesture, the knight's leg; it is not actually strapped round the pin-striped trouser. The Prelate, who is always the Bishop of Winchester, Windsor once being in his diocese, then pronounces the Admonition: 'To the Honour of God Omnipotent, and in Memorial of the Blessed Martyr, Saint George, tie about thy leg, for thy Renown, this Most Noble Garter; wear it . . . that hereby thou mayest be admonished to be courageous and having undertaken a just war . . . thou mayest stand firm, valiantly fight, courageously and successfully conquer'. The garter is one of the original insignia of the Order.

After the garter has been affixed, Black Rod presents the blue Riband of the Order which the Sovereign places over the left shoulder of the knight elect. This riband was introduced as part of the insignia by Charles II and superseded the narrow ribbon from which depended the Lesser George, a small representation of St George slaying the dragon – which had previously been worn.

The Star of the Order is next pinned to the knight elect's left breast and a further Admonition is pronounced this time by the Register, who is the Dean of Windsor. Thereafter the Sovereign places the Mantle on the shoulders of the knight elect and puts the collar, from which depends the Greater George over this, an Admonition being made at each investiture. Finally, the Register presents the new Knight with a Bible and administers the Oath by which the Knight swears to obey the Statutes of the Order and the Laws of the Realm.

After the ceremony lunch is served in the Waterloo Room. Towards the end of which we, the heralds, come into the picture, so I shall recount this part of the narrative in the first person.

For the past twenty years or so, most of the Officers of Arms have met for a picnic at Runnymede, together with those they have invited to attend the Service,

which takes place in the afternoon. The first to leave this jolly get-together are those who have tickets for standing on the grass outside St George's Chapel. They leave early to get the best positions for watching the procession, which will walk from the castle down to the chapel. Next we depart, as we have to be at the castle by 1.55 p.m. The last to leave are those with seats in the chapel, as the doors are not closed until 2.30.

When we arrive at the castle a military orchestra is playing outside the Waterloo Chamber where the Queen and her guests are lunching and have just about reached the pudding stage. Our dressing room is the room over the porch, but it is too early to put on our hot and heavy tabards, so we sit and gossip, or perambulate the State Rooms watching the crowds assembling in Engine Court just outside the castle. By 2.15 p.m. we are in our tabards and the Knights of the Garter, wearing morning coats decorated with the Star of the Order, emerge from lunch in a haze of cigar smoke and general euphoria to sign the attendance register and then be helped into their blue velvet mantles, lined with white taffeta and with the arms of the Order embroidered on the left shoulder.

It is then our job to marshal the procession in St George's Hall, so that when the Queen and those members of the Royal Family who belong to the Order enter at the far end, we are ready to lead them slowly down the staircase to the Grand Entrance.

Here the procession is met by the Constable and Governor of the Castle and the Military Knights of Windsor. These are not now knights, but retired senior officers. They are the successors in office to the twenty-four 'helpless and indifferent knights' who until the time of William IV, were known as the 'Poor Knights of Windsor'. Edward III instituted this body when he founded the Order, the idea being that they would receive food and lodging in return for attending on the Knights Companion, being present at Chapters of the Order and fulfilling the religious obligations of the knights. They still live in lodgings within the castle walls and attend services, but, on Garter Day, they wear their splendid scarlet uniforms and make a great contribution to the colourful procession, for they are followed by a detachment of the Yeoman of the Guard in full dress, between whom and the knights, we heralds walk, not exactly detracting from the splendour of the occasion in our richly embroidered tabards.

We proceed between lines of footguards and dismounted troopers of the household cavalry, their breast-plates gleaming, through Engine Court, under the Norman Gate and down the hill, through the Middle and Lower Wards of the castle, under the arch into the Horseshoe Cloister and then up the steps to the West door of the chapel, where we are met and preceeded by the ecclesiastical procession – the Sacristans, cross bearer, choristers, lay clerks, organist, minor canons, virger and canons of Windsor.

Outside it has been noisy and exciting. The crowds lining the carriageway down from the castle have been cheerful; clapping, cheering and waving, when not clicking their cameras and operating their cines. Two bands have been playing and, if it is very hot, some of the Household Cavalry may have fallen to the ground like tin soldiers, providing a macabre diversion for those who have waited sweating and sardine-like for two hours. In contrast, within the chapel all is still and cool. The congregation, mostly in formal dress, is silent. We walk down the nave, knowing that at the moment when we pass through the screen the silence will be torn apart by the glorious, emotive sound of a fanfare of trumpets, proclaiming that the Queen has now entered the chapel.

We go to our allotted places in the choir and the Queen stands facing the high altar. 'It is Our Pleasure', she says, 'that the Knight Companion newly Invested be Installed'. The Chancellor calls the new Knight's name and Garter conducts him to his stall, above which will be placed his crest and a banner of his arms until his death, and on the back of which will be fixed forever a brass plate enamelled with his full coat of arms as a perpetual memorial of his membership of the Order.

The Queen and the Chancellor are conducted to their stalls and the service begins. Towards the end the Register prays '. . . and to the Companions of this Most Noble Order give such virtue and grace, that thy name may be thereby magnified, the commonwealth be well served, and their good fame remain to their posterity . . .'. Then, after a final hymn, a brief prayer and the blessing, we follow the Military Knights out of the Chapel and line the steps leading down from the West Door to see members of the Royal Family return to the castle in carriages, and the knights in motor-cars. We, likewise, travel by motorcar, shed our tabards as quickly as we can and partake of a most welcome, excellent and elegant tea with others who have taken part in the ceremony, in the Waterloo Chamber. What happens after that is another story, but it has something to do with champagne. Yes, Garter Day is a great and joyous day and particularly so because so many people are able to crowd into the

Knights of the Order of the Garter walking in procession to St George's Chapel, Windsor, for the annual service of the Order in 1972.

castle precincts to witness it. It can be said to be England's official birthday.

I have dwelt on the Garter Service because the Garter is the oldest Order of Chivalry in Great Britain, the oldest Order of its kind in the world and because I have attended twenty-two Garter services as an Officer of Arms and enjoyed every one more than the last, except on the one occasion when it rained and the outside procession had to be called off. But what the Garter is to England the Thistle is to Scotland, and St Patrick used to be to Ireland.

The Thistle is officially known as The Most Ancient and the Most Noble Order of the Thistle. In fact, it is not so very ancient. James V of Scotland created the Order of St Andrew in 1540 which consisted of himself and twelve Knights Companion, in imitation of Christ and the twelve apostles. This Order fell into disuse at the Reformation, the Scottish Calvinists regarding such Orders as having papist origins.

The Catholic James VII (James II of England) 'revived' the Order in 1687, but called it the Order of the Thistle and dedicated it to St Andrew. The Order was not continued after James' involuntary abdication the following year, but Queen Anne promulgated Statutes and formally and finally revived the Order in 1703. Since 1821 the Order has consisted of the Sovereign, Royal Knights, Extra Knights (the only one is King Olave of Norway) and sixteen Knights Companion. The officers of the Order are the Chancellor, the Dean, the Secretary (Lyon King of Arms, the principal Scottish Herald) and the usher of the Green Rod. The chapel is a small building attached to St Giles' Cathedral, Edinburgh, and was built in 1911.

As with the Order of the Garter, there is a Thistle Service each year, at which the new knights, if there are to be any, are installed. St Giles' Cathedral is in Parliament Square opposite the imposing Signet Library, owned by the Writers to Her Majesty's Signet (a sort of Solicitors' Trades Union, only much much grander). On the day of the service the knights and the Scottish Officers of Arms, consisting of Lyon King of Arms, three heralds and three pursuivants, robe in this building, the knights donning their dark green velvet robes and bonnets, and form up to await the Queen and royal party, which drives up from the Palace of Holyrood in their robes.

A guard of honour of the Queen's Bodyguard for Scotland, The Royal Company of Archers, which is the equivalent of the Gentlemen at Arms in England, awaits them in Parliament Square. They enter the Signet Library and join the procession which the Officers of Arms lead across the square, through the cathedral and into the Thistle Chapel. Lyon and Green Rod lead the new knights to the Sovereign and then place them in their stalls, where they take the Oath. There follows a short service of prayers and readings, after which the procession is re-formed and goes back into the body of the cathedral for a further service before returning to the Signet Library, where, a Scottish Officer tells me, the Writers to the Signet very kindly provide them with some well-earned booze.

As there is not sufficient space in the Thistle Chapel to display the knights' banners these are hung in the Preston Aisle of the cathedral. However, their crests and Stall Plates are displayed in their chapel.

The Most Illustrious Order of St Patrick was founded in 1783 by George III. Unlike with the Garter and the Thistle, no appointments have been made to the Order since 1922 and there only remain the Sovereign and Norroy and Ulster King of Arms, who is also the Secretary and Knight Attendant. There are now no Knights Companion and the last Royal Knight was Henry Duke of Gloucester, who died in 1974.

The Orders I have described are different from the other Orders of Knighthood in that they are single-class Orders. All the members are simply Knights Companion; there are no other degrees.

Something has been said of the Order of the Bath. This Order has gone through many constitutional changes since it was revived, or, as we have seen, in fact established by George I in 1725. Originally, it was purely a military Order, but today there is a military and a civil division and it also consists of three classes – Knights and Dames Grand Cross, Knights and Dames Commanders, and Companions, who may be of either sex.

The chapel of the Order is Henry VII's magnificent chapel at the East end of Westminster Abbey, which makes a splendid setting for the installation of Knights Grand Cross who, like Garter Knights, display banners and have stall plates. As there are not stalls for all those with Grand Crosses they have to wait for a vacancy before being offered a stall. This is done in order of seniority – a question of dead men's shoes. Fortunately, as men do not receive this high honour in the bloom of their youth, the queue shuffles along at a reasonable pace.

The Queen has taken part in an Installation of Knights of the Bath, but usually the Great Master of the Order, the Prince of Wales, presides.

Opposite: *The Queen in the mantle of the Sovereign of the Most Distinguished Order of St Michael and St George, when attending a service at St Paul's Cathedral.*

The other Orders of Knighthood are, in order of seniority, the Star of India, which is obsolescent, the Royal Victorian Order and the Order of the British Empire. In these three Orders the first two classes are Knights and Dames Grand Cross and Knights and Dames. In the Orders of St Michael and St George there is a third, untitled class of Companions. The two remaining orders each have five classes, the last three being untitled.

The Orders of St Michael and St George and of the British Empire have their chapels in St Paul's Cathedral; the Royal Victorian Order uses the Queen's Chapel of the Savoy, but, unlike the other two Orders, no commemoration services are held.

How is it decided who shall receive this veritable treasure-trove of honours? In almost all cases, it is the Prime Minister who decides. However, the Sovereign still has three chivalric and two other Orders in her personal gift. These are the Order of Merit, the Royal Victorian Order, the Royal Victorian Chain and, since 1946 and 1947 respectively, the Garter and the Thistle.

Looking at some of the appointments which have been made to the two senior Orders and the Order of Merit, it looks as if the Queen may have had suggestions made to her, but the ultimate choice is essentially hers.

On 3 December 1946 it was officially announced 'The Prime Minister and the Leader of the Opposition have both accepted the view that the same procedure (that is as with the Order of Merit, which has always been in the royal gift) should apply to appointments of the Most Noble Order of the Garter in future. The King has been pleased to approve'. The same thing happened on 17 June 1947 with respect to the Thistle.

Apart from these few Orders, which are restricted to relatively few people, most other honours are announced biannually in lists known as the New Year Honours, and the Birthday Honours, the latter being published on the occasion of the Queen's Official Birthday in June.

Before these announcements lists of suggested honours have been sent to the Prime Minister's office. The bulk of these come from the Civil Service, Foreign and Commonwealth Office, the Armed Forces, Commonwealth Countries and the major political parties. Of course, there are smaller lists and a host of individuals recommending people, who are not infrequently themselves, for honours. The names of those recommended by political parties are scanned by the Political Honours Scrutiny Committee, at present presided over by Lord Shackleton. Others are sifted through by certain of the Prime Minister's staff.

When the names of 4000 or so lucky ones have been selected, a letter is sent from Downing Street to each of them saying that the Prime Minister 'has it in mind' to submit his or her name to the Queen 'with a recommendation that she may be graciously pleased to approve' such-and-such an honour. Before making the recommendation the Prime Minister would like to be assured that 'this mark of Her Majesty's favour was acceptable'. Well, in spite of the left-wing Mr William Hamilton's remark that the honours system aroused 'cynical hilarity' it seems that most people, if offered an honour, accept it and that those who refuse rarely do so as a matter of political principle, but because they consider the award insufficient.

When the honours have been announced, the recipients are invited to be invested with the insignia of their award. It is vastly to the Queen's credit that she personally invests as many recipients as is physically possible. Obviously, if she is away on a state visit abroad she has to delegate her responsibility as Fount of Honour in and the Commonwealth, she delegates to those with vice-regal authority, such as Governors General.

Investitures are held about twelve times a year in the ball room at Buckingham Palace. Those to be invested are invited to bring two friends or relatives. On arrival at the Palace, they ascend the Grand Staircase to the ornate and apparently windowless ball room, down either side are tiered benches and in the centre, rows of gilt chairs. At one end is the dais where the Queen and members of the household will stand, at the other end of the room an orchestra plays. The guests sit round the room and those to be invested, if their decoration is in the form of a medal hanging on the breast, have a little hook put on their coat lapel to avoid fumbling with pins, and are then sat in orderly rows on the little gilt chairs.

The Queen enters, the National Anthem is played and the first group to be honoured, having left the ball room, wait in a queue in a room to the left of the dais. As each person is moved forward he goes to the dais, bows and ascends the steps. The Queen confers the award and invariably says a few apt words before shaking hands with the recipient who bows, moves off to the right where, if he has a hook, it is removed, receives the box for his decoration and returns to his place. The arrangements and timing are perfect and seemingly effortless; the Queen is relaxed, friendly, yet dignified and it must be a very *blasé* person who does not come away with the feeling that he has been personally thanked and honoured by his Sovereign for service rendered to his country and this, when all is said and done, is the purpose of this simple, but moving and very personal ceremony.

Chapter 8

Funerals

Although the title of this chapter sounds rather lugubrious, the content is not, for it is about the pomp, circumstance and ceremony that, from time immemorial, has attended the laying to rest of poor and rich alike. Nothing could be more natural than that relatives and friends should wish to give their dead decent and dignified sepulture, nor that the Church should reverently bury those bodies which had once been the temples of the souls within them; sending those souls upon their final journey with all solemnity.

The Roman Catholic rite of burial which, until the Reformation, was the only rite performed in Britain, is filled with beauty and significance. No one can fail to be moved by it: the unbleached candles, the black vestments of the sacred ministers, the solemn chant, the haunting magic and finality of the *Dies Irae*, the final absolutions round the catafalque, when it is incensed and sprinkled with holy water and then, as the coffin is carried to the grave, the singing of that glorious hymn with its promise of resurrection, *In Paradisum* – 'May the angels lead thee into paradise, may the martyrs receive thee at thy coming, and lead thee to the holy city of Jerusalem. May the choir of angels receive thee and mayest thou have eternal rest with Lazarus, who once was poor'.

As all good Christian souls, whatever their condition, were sent to their reward with this mass of requiem, it is not surprising that the relatives of those who in life had been men of eminence and social standing, wished to bury them with added pomp. This was achieved by the development of what, for want of a better expression, may be called the lay ritual of burial. This consisted of an elaborate funeral procession in which the military emblems of the deceased were carried, accompanied by numerous mourners suitably habited. The coffin was draped with a rich funeral pall and awaited burial in a hearse, which was not a vehicle but an elaborate framework constructed to hold tapers and was hung with material richly decorated with heraldic emblems.

The Officers of Arms, from an early date, had the right to marshal funerals. Reference is made, in a document dated 1417, to heralds having no right to conduct a funeral without the licence of the first King (Garter) or the King of Arms of the Province (the two Provinces are respectively North and South of the river Trent) in which the funeral was to take place. This suggests that by the time of Henry V, it was the established practice for heralds to conduct funerals. The obvious reasons for this were that heralds were marshals of ceremonies and they also had a particular interest in the funerals of the gentry and nobility, at which their honours, such as banners, shields and crests, were carried. As we have seen, by the fifteenth century, the Officers of Arms, under the Constable and Marshal had complete control of the ordering of coats of arms.

The first detailed account of a heraldic funeral is that of the Earl of Salisbury and his son Sir Thomas Neville, who were buried at Bisham in Berkshire. On the day of the solemn mass the Kings of Arms and heralds brought the armorials of the deceased from the vestry, Garter carrying the coat, Clarenceux the shield, Windsor the sword and Chester the helm and crest, and placed themselves about the hearse. After the Gospel was read, the two Kings of Arms went to the West door of the church where there was a man astride a horse, covered with a trapper of arms, which they led to the door of the choir. At the offertory, the military emblems were handed by the Kings of Arms and heralds to the celebrant, who delivered them to the Earl of Warwick (he who was known to history as 'the Kingmaker'), the heir of the deceased. He

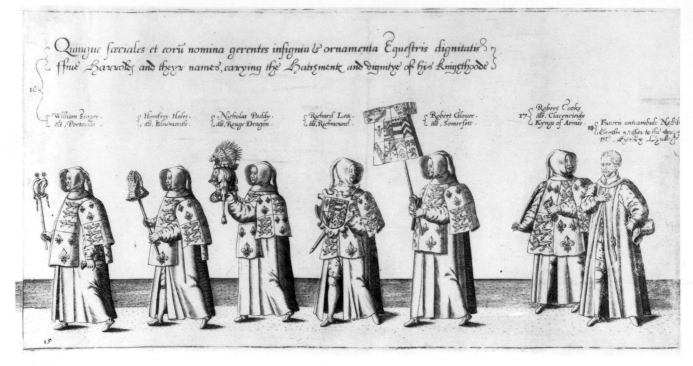

Heralds, wearing black mourning hoods, bearing the armorial insignia of Sir Philip Sydney in his funeral procession in 1584.

returned them to the Officers of Arms. The horse and trapper were offered to the church. Then the accoutrements were laid by the tomb and the Royal Officers, their job done, removed their tabards, but in token that the coat of arms was handed over by the heir's private herald, he kept his tabard on and stood before the hearse until the mass was ended. It is recorded that the Officers of Arms were well remunerated, the Kings receiving £3, plus 10s a day, the heralds £2 and 5s a day and the pursuivants £1 and 2s 6d a day, together with expenses, allowances, duties and fees. It is small wonder that the heralds were most concerned to establish and maintain a monopoly of conducting such funerals. Certainly, during the next hundred years heraldic funerals became popular even with the minor amorial gentry, especially the wealthy citizens of London.

Obviously, it would be contrary to the spirit of the age, indeed, probably of any age, for a London merchant to enjoy the same funeral pomp as a duke and so regulations were laid down as to exactly what was appropriate to each degree. For example, an earl might have nine mourners in his funeral procession, but a gentleman had to be content with three. The hearse of a duke was to be hung with velvet, the floor, but not the ceiling, with cloth decorated with escutcheons of taffeta, while the corpse rested on a *haute pace*. The pall was to be of seven breadths of velvet, the great standard eleven yards long and the banner four foot square. There were to be a guidon (small tapering flag), helm, crest, sword, targe (shield), gauntlets, spurs, coat of arms and eight banner-rolls (small banners). His coronet was to be carried on a cushion and there was to be a chief mourner, supported by two marquesses and attended by twelve assistants. A mourning horse and a horse of state were also permitted. A gentleman was restricted to a hearse ringed with baize and decorated with buckram escutcheons. He had a pall of five breadths of velvet, a pennon, but no banner nor standard, and a helm, crest and coat of arms, but no sword or spurs.

The Kings of Arms were also enjoined, by an Order of the Earl Marshal made in 1568, to take certificates from the relatives or executors of the deceased. These funeral certificates contained details of the death, burial, residence, marriage and issue of the defunct as well as a record of his or her arms and crest. It will be appreciated that funeral certificates can be valuable genealogical records and they are carefully preserved at the College of Arms. Funerals were lucrative, not only because of the fees and perquisites which accrued to the heralds, but also because fees were charged on taking certificates and because the armorial accoutre-

Opposite: The funeral accoutrements of Sir Charles Somerset, fifth son of Henry, Earl of Worcester, 1599.

m wynygard

Opposite: *The Choir of St George's Chapel, Windsor, with the banners of the Knights of the Garter hanging over their stalls.*

The funeral car bearing the coffin of Arthur, first Duke of Wellington, at his state funeral in 1852. The car is still preserved in the crypt of St Paul's Cathedral.

ments had to be specially made, funeral helms, crests, coats of arms and the like not being used in the late sixteenth and seventeenth centuries. These artefacts were supplied by the heralds, so attracting further profits. The heralds relentlessly pursued painters and craftsmen who were not employed by them and who threatened their monopoly by producing funeral accoutrements without the licence of a King of Arms.

After the Restoration of the Monarchy in 1660, the custom of holding heraldic funerals began to decline. There were but a handful of funeral certificates taken in the eighteenth century and, thereafter, there are only six which relate to State Funerals, that is funerals paid for by the State. These are the funerals of the first Earl Chatham, Viscount Nelson, Mr Gladstone, Earl Roberts, Viscount Alanbrooke and Sir Winston Churchill. William Pitt, second son of Lord Chatham, and the great Duke of Wellington also had public funerals which were attended by the heralds, but at which no certificates were taken.

The great State Funerals listed above, save perhaps that of Lord Chatham, only faintly reflected the elaborate, carefully regulated ceremonies of the preceeding centuries. They were, however, more awe-inspiring in their grandeur, reflecting the fame of those they honoured. At Lord Nelson's funeral, it is recorded that the Scots Greys, who led the procession, had reached St Paul's Cathedral before the rear of the procession had left the Admiralty. At the end of the

service, in the darkened cathedral, lit only by torches and a special chandelier, imported for the occasion, and holding 130 lamps, Sir Isaac Heard, Garter King of Arms, proclaimed the styles and titles of the great Admiral; the officers of his household broke the white wands of their office which Garter placed on the coffin before it was lowered into the crypt, where it now lies in a monstrous, but impressive tomb.

Of such a nature was the funeral of the late Sir Winston Churchill, which took place on 30 January 1965, although we – for it is the Earl Marshal and the Officers of Arms who arrange State Funerals – managed to introduce some elements from early heraldic funerals.

It all began some five years before Sir Winston died. At that time his health seemed uncertain and it was the wish of the Queen and the Prime Minister to offer him the signal honour of a State Funeral. His son, the late Mr Randolph Churchill, was deputed to ask his father if he wanted such a splendid farewell. He did: guns, trumpets, soldiers, the lot! From that moment, discreetly and secretly, we began to plan what was code-named 'Operation Hope Not'.

The particular care of the Officers of Arms was the seating in St Paul's Cathedral and, of course, the actual ceremonial. As may be imagined, we trod on delicate ground because, being a State Funeral, the Nation and Foreign Nations had to be widely represented but, at the same time, the wishes and

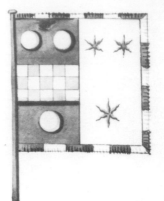

The Coronet on a black

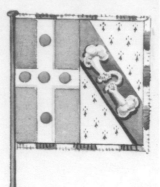

The
BODY
Covered with a black
Velvet Pall adorned with
eight Escocheons of the
Arms of the deceased,
and under a Canopy of
black Velvet borne by
eight Gentlemen.

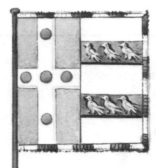

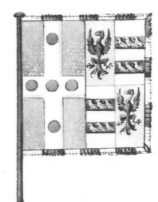

sensitivities of the family had to be respected and all this when the object of the operation was still alive. Fortunately, the family could not have been more helpful and co-operative. They appreciated that Sir Winston belonged to the Free World and that his family would simply be joining with others in paying their last respects to the old warrior when the good Lord called him. I can truly say that the family were the least of our worries and, when it was all over, those of us who had been concerned with the arrangements received a present from Lady Spencer-Churchill. I was sent Sir Winston's *A History of the English-Speaking Peoples*, inscribed 'with my thanks, Clementine S. Churchill'. I treasure this, both for what it is and also because it serves as a perpetual reminder of a day when sorrow was transcended by national pride, a day when every Briton and many from all over the world were able to acclaim and pay homage to a national and international hero.

During those five years of 'hoping not' we worked on the Ceremonial, on the categories of people who should be invited and amassed the necessary stationery. In all this no reference was made to Sir Winston. The tickets, ceremonials and so forth simply referred to a 'State Funeral'. Our headquarters was an attic in the College of Arms, in Queen Victoria Street – the 'Hope Not Attic'.

While we were doing this, the police were making provisional arrangements for duty rotas and parking and traffic control, and the General Officer Commanding London District and his staff worked on the outside processions and street lining.

Perhaps all this sounds a little macabre, but the date of a man's death is as uncertain as it is certain that he will die, and we wanted Sir Winston's funeral to be a ceremony of which the British and especially Sir Winston, could be proud. It was necessary, therefore, to do as much discreet advance planning as was seemly and possible. After all, a mediaeval grandee as often as not laid down careful instructions for the disposal of his mortal remains and, perhaps not trusting his heirs, even had his tomb prepared in advance. Sir Winston, who was a twentieth century grandee, always took an interest in our tactful exertions on his behalf.

Naturally, we wanted heraldry to play a traditional role in the funeral pomp and we achieved this in the following way. In the outside procession from Westminster Hall, where the body had lain in State, to

Part of the official record of the funeral of William Pitt, first Earl Chatham, in 1778. The banners represent alliances of the Pitt family and of Lady Chatham's family.

St Paul's Cathedral, the Banner of the arms of the Cinque Ports (three lions of England, their bodies cut in half and joined to the hulks of ancient ships) was borne alternately by two officers of The Queen's Royal Irish Hussars. Likewise, two officers of the same regiment, of which Sir Winston was Colonel, bore the banner of the arms of Spencer-Churchill alternately. In front of the banner bearers four other officers bore the orders and decorations of the deceased on velvet cushions. It may seem surprising that four cushions were required, but apart from having the Order of the Garter, the Order of Merit, the Order of the Companion of Honour, and a great number of campaign medals, Sir Winston also sported a glittering galaxy of foreign honours.

On arrival at the cathedral, the officers bearing the deceased's banners and honours joined the Officers of Arms who were waiting there, four of whom carried further honours, namely, Sir Winston's spurs, sword, crest and targe (that is his shield). It is interesting to note that these honours usually had to be purpose-made for a seventeenth century funeral but this was not so in Sir Winston's case. The sword and spurs were his own, the banner was that which had been displayed over his Garter Stall in St George's Chapel, as was the crest; only the shield had to be prepared specially for the occasion.

Apart from seeing that heraldry was not forgotten, the funeral was arranged on traditional lines but we did revive a rather interesting custom. Naturally, like everyone else, we wore mourning bands on our sleeves, but, as these were obscured when we donned our tabards, diagonally across these we put on black mourning sashes. As far as I can discover these had only been used on one previous occasion, at the funeral in 1817 of Princess Charlotte of Saxe-Coburg, Duchess of Kendal, and George IV's only daughter.

The actual order of proceeding is probably best described in the terse, but factual words contained in the Special District Order of Major General E.J.B. Nelson, G.O.C., London District. 'The Coffin of Sir Winston Churchill will be taken in Procession in Slow Time from Westminster Hall to St Paul's Cathedral.

After a Service in St Paul's Cathedral the Procession will continue in Slow Time to Tower Pier where the Coffin will be embarked in a Launch in which it will be conveyed up the River Thames.

The processional route will be lined by troops of the three Services. Minute Guns will be fired during the progress of the procession. Guards of Honour will be mounted by the Royal Navy, the Royal Marines, the Brigade of Guards and the Royal Air Force. A fly-past will be carried out by the Royal Air Force. A 17-Gun-Salute will be fired from Her Majesty's Tower.

Sir Winston Churchill's coffin being carried from St Paul's Cathedral after the funeral service.

Having left Tower Pier, the Coffin will be taken to Festival Hall Pier from where it will be conveyed by Motor Hearse to Waterloo Station. After a Train journey to Long Hanborough Station the Coffin will be taken by Motor Hearse for Interment at Bladon'.

Although that is literally what happened, it hardly captures the drama of that historic day. The outside procession was all Sir Winston could ever have wished it to be. It was led by detachments from all the armed services, interspersed by eight bands. At the head of the procession were Battle of Britain Air Crews and at the end, before the Earl Marshal's procession, the first detachment of the Household Cavalry.

The Earl Marshal's procession was led by the Chiefs of the Air Staff, Naval Staff and General Staff, followed by Admiral of the Fleet and Earl Mountbatten of Burma, Chief of the Defence Staff.

Then came the honour and banner bearers, followed by senior officers from London District and the Earl Marshal.

Behind the Earl Marshal came the gun carriage bearing the coffin between two detachments of a Royal Naval Gun Crew. As with any funeral, the family and principal mourners followed the coffin. Behind them rode the second detachment of the Household Cavalry, two bands and contingents from the Police, Fire Services and Civil Defence Corps.

For an hour the slow procession wound its way up Whitehall, along the Strand and Fleet Street and then up Ludgate Hill and to St Paul's Cathedral. We were standing, fanned out on the steps, our knees shaking a little as the bitter cold penetrated our silk stockings. Anxiously we watched as the bearer party lifted the coffin, draped with the Union Flag and surmounted by a velvet cushion on which were the Collar, Star and Garter of the Most Noble Order of the Garter.

For a moment it looked at though one of the bearers was going to faint; an officer moved forward, but fortunately the man recovered himself and we led the procession up the nave of the cathedral. Behind us walked the twelve Pall Bearers, most of whose names were part of the nation's history – Macmillan, Menzies, Templer, Normanbrook, Bridges, Ismay, Slim, Portal of Hungerford, Avon, Atlee, Alexander of Tunis and Mountbatten of Burma. As we passed the Queen and members of the Royal Family I thought how strange it was not to be leading them, but for that one day we had, as it were, been lent to Sir Winston. The Queen's name did not even appear in the *Order of Ceremonial*. Yet she made history, for she was the first British Sovereign to be a principal mourner at a Prime Minister's funeral.

We took up our places, forming a line in front of the choir, our tabards providing one of the few splashes of colour in that sombre gathering. Then the service began. It was a rousing, splendid, triumphant service. In the words and tunes of all the hymns the nature of the man we were honouring was captured. 'Who would true valour see', 'Mine eyes have seen the glory of the coming of the Lord', 'Fight the good fight with all thy might', and then, as we led the procession back down the nave, the singing of 'O God, our help in ages past' made voices crack with emotion and eyes dampen with tears, but they were tears of pride rather than sorrow, for he was one of us.

After the ceremony we stood on the steps for at least twenty minutes as the representatives of foreign nations slowly departed. I remember thinking at the time that one of the things we British can be proud of is our security. There on the steps, in full view of the crowds and the buildings surrounding St Paul's, were most of the Royal Family, the Kings of Norway and Greece, the Queen of the Netherlands, President de Gaulle of France, the Presidents of Israel, Iceland, Zambia and many other notables, yet there were no strong-arm men, no bullet-proof cars, no escorts of roaring motorcycles. For all the world that group, exposed on the steps, might have been a troop of boy-scouts so efficiently and discreetly do our security officers do their work. The Earl Marshal was highly and rightly incensed when a certain representative of a foreign (and friendly) nation asked if he could have twelve armed guards in the cathedral. The answer was terse – 'No'. The representative did not come.

On this occasion, as on other State occasions, special ushers were appointed to show people to their seats and control their departure. They were called Purple Staff Officers and carried appropriately col-

oured staves. Those of us concerned with seating were on duty to sort out any problems which might arise until the doors were closed at 10 a.m. At that time we went and put on our tabards and no one else could be admitted – at least, almost no one. Just after ten a knock was heard at one of the great doors of the cathedral. A policeman opened it and outside were two men who had forgotten their tickets. The policeman asked what category they were. One replied that he was a Prime Minister. At which the policeman no doubt smiled cynically as if to say 'and I'm the Emperor of Japan', but he let them in, holding them until someone came and identified them. They turned out to be Mr Ian Smith and his *aide de camp*.

'Did you rehearse it?' is a question I am often asked, usually in a tone which suggests the unspoken rider 'because surely it is indecent to rehearse a funeral'. Well, there is something in that sentiment, but this was no ordinary funeral. It was a great public spectacle and people wanted it to be perfect, nothing less would do for 'their' hero. So, yes, we rehearsed. There were small rehearsals of both outside and inside processions and procedures, but only one big combined rehearsal of all outside processions, other than at Waterloo Station, and that was held at 4.45 a.m. on a dark winter morning, so as to attract as little attention as possible.

A few weeks after it was all over, I and others received a letter of thanks from the Earl Marshal. The second paragraph of his letter to me read:

> However, this is to thank you and through you, all your people who helped my staff and myself so greatly at the time of the funeral of the late Sir Winston Churchill. It was only through the great co-operation I received that we achieved what appears to have been acknowledged as a successful event.

A splendid example of British understatement!

The funeral of a sovereign is similar to that which I have described, but less triumphant and it follows a known and accepted pattern.

The body of the deceased monarch lies in state in Westminster Hall for about four days and is then taken in procession to Paddington Station and thence by train to Windsor, where the committal service is semi-private. The ceremony is arranged by the Earl Marshal, who obviously receives a great deal of help and support from the Lord Chamberlain's Office, which looks after all domestic royal ceremonies, including funerals of members of the Royal Family, for these are not State Funerals.

The Officers of Arms take part in the actual ceremonies in St George's Chapel, Windsor and Garter King of Arms proclaims the late sovereign's

titles, but as the chapel is small there cannot be a great service like that which took place in St Paul's.

Perhaps this is as well, as we could not be expected to be forever planning a great State Funeral for the sovereign. The Royal Family tend to want as much privacy as possible and in theory the heir to the throne has the disposal of the body of his predecessor, so might want the most modest funeral possible.

The Duke of Windsor wrote in *A King's Story* that when his father died at Sandringham 'it came to my mind that my father would have preferred his earthly remains to be spared the huge State funeral and [be] buried in the Peaceful churchyard at Sandringham. But Windsor claims the bodies of British Monarchs'. So, even in death, the people's wishes come before those of the Sovereign's own kin.

Chapter 9

Jubilees and Durbars

Philologists are uncertain as to the true origin of the word jubilee, but there are no doubts regarding the origin of royal jubilees.

We read in the twenty-fifth Chapter of the Book of Leviticus:

> And thou shalt number seven sabbaths of years unto thee, seven times seven years; and the space of the seven sabbaths of years shall be unto thee forty and nine years.
>
> Then shalt thou cause the trumpet of the jubile to sound on the tenth *day* of the seventh month, in the day of atonement shall ye make the trumpet sound throughout all your land.
>
> And ye shall hallow the fiftieth year and proclaim liberty throughout *all* the land unto all the inhabitants thereof: it shall be a jubile unto you; and ye shall return every man unto his possession, and ye shall return every man unto his family.
>
> A Jubile shall that fiftieth year be unto you . . . it shall be holy unto you . . .

There follows a detailed account of how property and Hebrew slaves may be redeemed in the year of jubile and also other customs that shall be observed. After the exile of the Jews into Egypt the Levitical Law of keeping jubilees seems no longer to have been followed, although they were 'reckoned'.

The idea of a jubilee was revived in 1300 by Pope Boniface VIII who proclaimed a jubilee year during which pilgrims to Rome could obtain plenary indulgences upon certain conditions, including a visit to either the Basilica of Saint Peter or Saint Paul. Boniface's plan was that a jubilee should be held every hundred years. However, the Romans persuaded Pope Clement VI to reduce the period to fifty years (one suspects from motives of gain rather than piety) which he obligingly did and a jubilee was held in 1350. Having got the bit between their teeth the Romans

decided that even fifty years was too long to wait for the spiritual and material fruits which a jubilee brought them and Urban VI proclaimed the next jubilee thirty-three years ater the 1350 jubilee. Thirty-three years was supposed to be the length of Christ's sojourn on earth. Finally, Pope Paul II (1464–1471) fixed the interval at twenty-five years and so it has remained ever since. The last jubilee, now usually called a Holy Year, was celebrated in 1975.

When George III had reigned for fifty years the idea of holding a royal Golden Jubilee was not considered, probably because of the King's periodic fits of insanity, but it was thought to be a fitting way of celebrating Queen Victoria's fifty years on the throne, in 1887.

The timing, although it was ineluctable, happened to be impeccable. The Queen was just beginning to emerge from her seemingly everlasting period of mourning for her late husband, Prince Albert, who had been dead for over twenty-five years, and it would greatly boost the waning prestige of the monarchy if she made a really significant public appearance.

In 1887 the mood of the country was changing; there was less real poverty, more people had more money, the British flag flew high throughout the world and Disraeli's Imperialism or, as his opponents called it, Jingoism, had caught the imagination of a large section of the population. If ever there were a time to celebrate, this was it.

The great ceremony was not officially classified as a State Ceremony, so the Lord Chamberlain of the Household, the Earl of Lathom, was in charge of the arrangements, although most of the actual work would have been undertaken by the Comptroller of the Lord Chamberlain's Office, the Honourable Sir Spencer Ponsonby-Fane.

Although Victoria's Golden Jubilee was the first

ever celebrated, there had been a similar celebration, albeit on a very reduced scale, in 1872. In the Queen's Speech opening Parliament, she had announced her intention of holding a service of thanksgiving in St Paul's Cathedral for the recovery of the Prince of Wales from typhoid, more delicately described as 'his late dangerous illness'.

On the 27 February, the day fixed for the service, the Queen drove in State to St Paul's, performing at Temple Bar the ceremony of accepting from and returning to the Lord Mayor of London, the City Sword.

Benjamin Disraeli, Earl of Beaconsfield, a great imperialist and friend of Queen Victoria.

At St Paul's the Queen was met by various members of her Household, including Lancaster, Somerset and Chester Heralds (all incorrectly designated in the official ceremonial) and Norroy and Garter Kings of Arms. The rest of the heralds were given tickets to enable them and their guests to attend, but were not included in the proceedings.

After the service, which followed 'the Form ordered by Her Majesty's Privy Council' the Queen returned to Buckingham Palace by a different and longer route than the direct route she had taken to the cathedral, 'in order to meet the loyal wishes of Her Subjects'. Crowds assembled in the streets, which were lined by personnel from a great variety of

regiments and corps as well as by 400 sailors. At the service there were a few foreign guests, among them Prince Hassan of Egypt and Prince Higashi-Fushimi-No-Miya of Japan, the *Corps Diplomatique*, peers, peeresses and peers' eldest sons, members of the House of Commons, Lords Lieutenant and High Sheriffs of Counties, Mayors and Provosts of the United Kingdom, and representatives of the universities, medical professions, nonconformist bodies, the Civil Service and of many other bodies selected to represent the nation. In all 13,000 people attended the service in St Paul's. This ceremony must have provided the Lord Chamberlain's Office with a blue-print of a fairly considerable ceremony, which would have helped to guide it in 1887.

The principal differences between the thanksgiving and the jubilee ceremonies was that the former took place in St Paul's while the jubilee service was held in Westminster Abbey and on the latter occasion an unbelievable number of foreign royals and representatives of foreign nations attended and had to be housed, looked after and entertained. For example, the Prince Devawongse Varoprakar of Siam, who stayed at the Alexandra Hotel had two English 'bear-leaders' to look after him, as well as his two Military Attachés and the First Secretary of the Siamese Legation. In addition to this host of foreigners, a large number of Indian Princes attended with their suites and indeed they were quite a feature of the jubilee celebrations in their magnificent robes, their turbans glittering with jewels. In all there were forty-four carriages in the procession from and back to the Palace, which gives some idea of the number of notables who attended.

The use of Westminster Abbey rather than St Paul's meant that considerable works, similar to those carried out before a coronation, had to be undertaken by the Board of Works in order to accommodate the guests, for the Abbey is a much smaller church than St Paul's, quite apart from being cluttered up with monuments making it more like a pantheon than a place of worship.

Although the Queen was suffering from rheumatism, disliked tiring ceremonies and never went to London if she could avoid it, she entered into the spirit of the occasion more than anyone had dared to expect. She proclaimed Jubilee Day a public holiday, remitted prison sentences, pardoned all those who had 'deserted or absented themselves without leave from Our Regular Forces, Militia or Reserved Forces, or having fraudulently enlisted' and she relaxed Court etiquette to allow ladies, who were innocent parties in divorce cases, to be admitted to Court. She wanted to extend this clemency to foreign ladies, but Lord

Salisbury advised her not to be so rash because of the danger of admitting 'American women of light character'.

The Queen even evinced her interest by making a personal visit to the Abbey to see how everything was getting on. 'Big deal!' one might be tempted to mutter, but it must be remembered that the Queen had become a complete recluse, morbidly pre-occupied with her grief. Only a year before she had refused to prorogue Parliament in person, on the grounds that her presence would be used to make political capital. An excuse which incited Gladstone to write to her Private Secretary '. . . smaller and meaner causes for the decay of Thrones cannot be conceived'.

Where the Queen did draw the line was at wearing robes and the Crown and carrying the Sceptre. In spite of the Prince of Wales' blandishments and the advice of Lord Rosebery and Lord Halifax, she was adamant and the only royal symbol displayed was her Parliamentary Robe, which was draped over the Coronation Chair used by her during the service.

Although the Queen's decision not to wear regalia was made on personal grounds, it turned out to be the right decision from a purely theatrical point of view. Had she worn robes and crown, the diminutive, dumpy little woman would have been eclipsed by her gloriously clad subjects and foreign guests, splendid in a variety of colourful uniforms and national costumes and ablaze with a multitude of Orders. As it was, she stood out dramatically because she was the only person dressed simply in black, relieved only by the stars of the Order of the Garter and the Star of India.

When the service was over the Princes and Princesses who had been sitting behind the Queen on a raised dais came and kissed her hand and were embraced by her. The Queen then left in procession for Buckingham Palace where luncheon was served in the Supper Room at 3.45 p.m. After lunch, the Queen received various loyal addresses and presents and in the evening gave a 'Full Dress Banquet to Her Royal and Princely Guests, and the Royal Family'. It is interesting to note that the Indian Princes, Queen Kapiolani and Princess Liliyewokalani, Prince Komatsu of Japan and the Siamese and Persian Princes were not invited to the banquet, but were received by the Queen afterwards.

The jubilee celebrations did not end that night. The next day the Queen spent the whole morning going from room to room in Buckingham Palace receiving gifts and loyal addresses from such diverse bodies as the Citizens of Worcester, the Royal Female School of Art and the Fox Court Ragged School. In the afternoon she went to a fête in Hyde Park, attended by 30,000 London school children. Then she travelled by train from Paddington to Slough where there were more loyal addresses and presentations; thence to Eton and Windsor and a dinner party in the Castle. After dinner, nine hundred boys comprising fourteen companies of Eton Volunteers carrying torches and lanterns, entertained the Queen and her guests with music and songs and by making formations, such as the letters 'V.R.' with their torches. At the end of the display the Queen said 'I am very grateful for the welcome you have given me, and sincerely thank you for this beautiful sight'. It must have been quite a day for the old lady.

For a further six weeks the Queen continued her arduous round of duties. There were State banquets galore, innumerable loyal addresses and gifts were presented and graciously accepted, the Fleet was reviewed, a garden party given and several investitures held and, on Monday, 4 July, the Queen laid the first stone of the Imperial Institute, in a very large pavilion specially erected for the purpose.

This was a considerable ceremony, attended by foreign guests and members of the Royal Family. The Queen drove in state from Paddington to Exhibition Road, where she was met by the Prince of Wales, whose brain-child the Institute was. A procession was formed which, in composition, was not unlike that at the Opening of Parliament. It went by covered way to the pavilion where it was greeted by a fanfare of trumpets followed by a processional march played by an orchestra under the direction of Sir Arthur Sullivan. The actual ceremony must have been infinitely boring. The Prince of Wales read a long address to the Queen, who replied suitably. Then, with the help of her son, she deposited a statement concerning the origin of the Institute and a set of newly minted coins, under a stone. She then laid the first stone, 'being assisted in the use of the line and plummet by T.E. Collcutt, Esq., The Architect'. After which there was a further long address and response, the proceedings ending with a Benediction from the Archbishop of Canterbury and the singing of 'Rule Britannia'.

What is interesting from a herald's point of view is that, while we were almost totally neglected at the jubilee service, only Garter King of Arms and Lancaster and Windsor Heralds being in attendance, at the Imperial Institute ceremony all the Officers of Arms attended in levee dress and took part in the procession, the pursuivants leading.

The British, like the Romans, seem to have acquired a taste for jubilees, for they invented a special one to celebrate a reign of sixty years and called it a Diamond Jubilee. The Queen, who had been much

more active since her Golden Jubilee, had regained the affection and admiration of her people at home and in the ever-expanding Empire. Her reign was everywhere referred to as the Victorian period; her name had become part of the language. There was much to celebrate, and enthusiasm for the 1897 jubilee was even greater than for the previous one, perhaps because the first jubilee was imposed from above whereas the next had its roots in the spontaneous emotions of the people. The fantastic and elaborate decorations of London, the uncriticized expenditure of considerable sums of money and the influx of visitors from all over the world bear witness to the ground swell of real fervour.

Mr Joseph Chamberlain, the Colonial Secretary, who had once called for the abolition of the mon-archy, was keen to make political capital out of the jubilee by inviting Colonial Prime Ministers and detachments of troops from all over the Empire to participate in the ceremonies in place of crowned heads. To this suggestion the Queen readily agreed, particularly as it meant that she would not have to invite her son-in-law, the German Emperor, whom she detested.

The imperial character of the jubilee militated towards it being a resounding success. The crowds loved the Imperial Forces and also the idea of being part of a great and growing community of people. Exactly the right note was struck. Sir Walter Besant wrote prophetically in the jubilee number of *The Illustrated London News*, 'there have arisen four great nations – Canada, Australia, South Africa and

George V and Queen Mary, walking in state at the great Durbar or Court which was held at Delhi, soon to be proclaimed the Capital of India, in 1911.

New Zealand – any one of which must in the nature of things become, nominally if not actually more and more independent. The great problem of the immediate future will be not only the preservation of the States under the Union Jack, but the preservation of friendship and alliance of all four; with the Mother Country first and with each other next'.

The jubilee was the point of departure for tackling the problem envisaged by Sir Walter.

I will not describe the actual ceremony. It was a long and grand proceeding through the packed streets of London, as on the previous occasion. The main difference was that the thanksgiving service which was very brief took place in front of St Paul's Cathedral and not in the Abbey.

The Queen recorded in her journal 'A never-to-be-forgotten day. No one ever, I believe, has met with such an ovation as was given to me, passing through those six miles of streets . . . The crowds were quite indescribable, and their enthusiasm truly marvellous and deeply touching . . . the denseness of the crowds was immense, but the order maintained wonderful'.

Sir Walter Besant made no reference to that 'brightest jewel' in the Crown, which was one day to become a thorn in the flesh of the Empire – India. However, King George V did not forget it. At his suggestion, after his coronation at Westminster, he

and Queen Mary embarked for India on the Peninsular and Oriental vessel *Medina* on 11 November 1911, there to be acclaimed as King-Emperor and Queen-Empress at a great durbar or court.

It must have been a poignant moment for the royal couple as the roar of the guns of the Home Fleet bidding them farewell and safe return died away, for many had expressed doubts at the wisdom of the visit, prophesying that the King and Queen might never come back alive. Which is perhaps why, when they did return safely, they at once attended a thanksgiving service in St Paul's Cathedral.

On 2 December the King-Emperor landed at Bombay, the first reigning sovereign ever to set foot on Indian soil. The Imperial camp, which covered twenty-five square miles, was three miles from the vast amphitheatre at Delhi where the great durbar, one of the most magnificent ceremonies ever held in the colourful East, took place on 12 December.

The Occasion is probably best described in the King's own words, quoted by John Gore in *King George V*:

> May and I were photographed before we started in our robes, I wore the same clothes and robes as at the Coronation with a new Crown made for India which cost £60,000, which the Indian Government is going to pay for. We left camp at 11.30 . . . in an open carriage . . . the whole way to the Amphitheatre lined with troops. The Amphitheatre contained about 12,000 people, there were some 18,000 troops inside it and over 50,000 people on the Mount. On our arrival we took our seats on the thrones facing the centre of the crescent. I first made a speech giving the reasons for holding the Durbar, then the Governor General did homage to me, followed by all the Ruling Chiefs, Governors, Lieut-Governors and members of the different Councils. We then walked in procession . . . to two other silver thrones raised upon a platform facing the troops and the Mound. The Heralds rode into the Amphitheatre and the Chief Herald, Gen. Peyton, read the Proclamation (which the Assistant Herald read in Urdu). Then the Governor General read a paper announcing the boons . . . We returned in procession to the first thrones when I announced that the Capital will be transferred from Calcutta to Delhi, the ancient capital . . . the whole people present then sung the National Anthem and the most wonderful Durbar ever held was closed. . . .

The reference to the two heralds is interesting. They were not regular Officers of Arms appointed to

Opposite: George V and Queen Mary driving up Ludgate Hill to St Paul's Cathedral in their carriage in 1935 to attend the Thanksgiving Service on the occasion of their Silver Jubilee.

attend upon the Sovereign and so get a free trip to India, but extraordinary heralds appointed for the occasion. One, as the King noted, was General William Peyton and the other was a Punjabi chief (Tiwana), Sir Malik Mohammed Amur Khan. Although they were given no heraldic titles they wore tabards at the durbar.

The next day, robed as before, the royal couple attended the durbar garden party, sitting on the balcony of Shah Jehan's Palace, so that all might see them. There was also a review of British and Indian troops and an investiture at which the Queen-Empress received the Order of the Star of India, kneeling before her husband. After many other ceremonial appearances and a jolly tiger shoot, which seems to have been more photographed than the durbar itself, the King and Queen returned to Britain. From the point of view of royal prestige the reign had been well launched. The new King might not be the jolly, hard-living, fun-loving fellow his father had been, but he was a brave and conscientious man. As it turned out, he had just the qualities that were needed in the difficult years that lay ahead.

The monarchy survived these years, but had it failed to do so, it would not have been the fault of the King and Queen; it would have been because millions of hungry, unemployed people tend to act emotionally and erratically and there was a time when they could have toppled the monarchy, seeing it through tired, famished eyes as an unnecessary extravagance.

As the economy improved, criticism of the monarchy receded and the Silver Jubilee (yet another variety of jubilee, celebrating a reign of twenty-five years, having been conceived) was celebrated with wild enthusiasm in 1935. I think people liked the King because his prejudices were theirs and his virtues those they admired. He disliked Germans, homosexuals and place-seekers and once referred to Ghandi as 'this rebel fakir', sentiments shared by most of his subjects. He was a completely honest man who put duty first; he loved the simple country life and country pursuits and was in no way a social snob; he chose his friends because he liked them. So the jubilee was a great success. The King and Queen celebrated it with the usual drive to St Paul's, where a service was held and then, in the weeks following, they made many drives into the London suburbs where everywhere, even in the poorest areas, the streets were hung with bunting. The whole of London – the whole country – was *en fête*.

The arrangements for celebrating the Queen's Silver Jubilee in 1977 were similar to those in 1935. As a herald, all I had to do was to be present in my tabard, with my brother officers, in St Paul's for the thanksgiving service.

It was an extremely uncomfortable occasion as we were all squashed into a row of tightly packed small chairs and were more or less interlocked and unable to move in our tabards. It all seemed a little undignified; I felt we should have stood, facing the Sovereign as at Sir Winston's Funeral and as four of us did at the service held to mark the 750th anniversary of the sealing of *Magna Carta* in 1964.

As Chairman of my local District Queen's Silver Jubilee Fund Committee, I saw the jubilee in a different light, but one which was equally interesting. In my opinion the event had been anticipated too far in advance by commercial concerns and this had built up a certain reserve, if not an actual resentment, to the occasion; but it was superficial resentment because as the great day drew nearer, there was a sudden burst of frenetic activity to express the deep loyalty and sense of gratitude which most people felt towards the Queen. In my own village it seemed as if the jubilee might pass almost unnoticed but Jubilee Day turned out to be one of the most joyful days in the history of the village. Bunting suddenly appeared from nowhere, the jubilee dinner was a sell-out and people danced in the big barn until the small hours.

So it was everywhere. Television enabled millions to be with the Queen in St Paul's and then to let their hair down, forget their British reserve and celebrate as a nation, with a touch of arrogance, the fact that they like being what they are and being the subjects of the Queen rather than numbers in the computer of a faceless republic.

Chapter 10

The Machinery of Monarchy

The Royal Household is that small body of men and women who look after the Queen, both as a person and as Head of State. Her ceremonial functions, her royal tours, her official and private residences, her patronage, both lay and ecclesiastical – all and much more are attended to by the various departments of the Royal Household.

The list of senior members of the Household reads rather like the cast of a Victorian pantomime. There is the Lord Great Chamberlain, the Master of the Horse, the Lord Steward, the Master of the Queen's Musick (never forget the final 'k') and the Hereditary Grand Almoner. Most of these are noblemen who could never be expected to supervise the day-to-day affairs of the Household. They are of course no more than traditional appointments and their active roles are more or less confined to ceremonial appearances: the actual business of the Household is entrusted to paid, permanent officers.

However, in essence, the running of the Household is still conducted on traditional lines, although these have been rationalized considerably. There are three principal departments of the Household: those of the Lord Steward, the Lord Chamberlain and the Master of the Horse.

The department of the Lord Steward, who is the Duke of Northumberland, is responsible for the domestic economy. In practical terms this means looking after the day-to-day running of the Queen's five residences, Buckingham Palace, Windsor Castle, the Palace of Holyroodhouse, Balmoral Castle and Sandringham, although only the last two actually belong to the Queen. Also in his care are the finances of the Household. For these reasons his department is sometimes called the 'below stairs department'.

Prince Albert, when he married Queen Victoria, was horrified to discover how hopelessly inefficient was the running of the Lord Steward's department and he decided to do something about it. As he had been warned off meddling in State affairs he busied himself with domestic chores. Not unnaturally he encountered much hostility from those who were happily enjoying sinecures and living off the royal bounty, without the Queen actually knowing that she was dispensing it. In the end he was successful and it is to him that the Master of the Household owes his office.

The Master of the Household is a paid officer who acts as the Queen's 'housekeeper'. It is he who hires and fires all domestic staff, arranges menus, orders food and drink for both guests and staff, presides over the Board of Green Cloth and is responsible for a host of other details conducive to the smooth running of the royal domestic economy in the Queen's Houses. All this he does in the name of the Lord Steward and with the help of an efficient staff of clerks, housekeepers and other assistants. I have presumed to call his staff efficient because I have never noticed the Master of the Household being anything but cool, calm and urbane; one with such an unfurrowed brow must have confidence that he has a really first-rate team working for him.

The Queen's finances are controlled by the Keeper of the Privy Purse and Treasurer. It is he who is responsible for dispensing the annual sum voted to the Queen by Parliament and known as the Civil List. This money is not, as critics of the monarchy often try to insinuate, a personal salary. George III, in 1760, gave the revenues from the Crown Lands to Parliament in exchange for a fixed sum; this sum is

Opposite: The Queen after distributing the Royal Maundy at Westminster Abbey on 19 April 1973 accompanied by the Dean of Westminster.

The Queen's landau driving down the course at Ascot before the Royal flat race meeting.

The Queen and the Duke of Edinburgh accompanied by the Prince of Wales and Princess Anne during the Royal Ascot meeting in an open landau in 1972.

known as the Civil List. Out of it the Queen must pay all salaries, the cost of travelling, entertaining, public engagements (the royal garden parties alone must cost in excess of £65,000) both at home and overseas – in short, it must cover almost the whole expense of ceremonial and constitutional monarchy. Contrary to popular belief, the cost of our monarchy is probably less than many non-executive presidencies and a mere drop in the ocean compared with the cost of electing and maintaining the Chief Executive of the United States.

The Queen has, of course, her private fortune, in which she takes a personal interest, the Royal Almonry being looked after by her Treasurer. Although there is an Hereditary Grand Almoner, the Marquess of Exeter; a High Almoner, the Bishop of Rochester; and a Sub-Almoner, Canon Anthony Caesar, this is a small department, of whose activities the public becomes aware once a year on Maundy Thursday. On this occasion the Queen, accompanied by the High Almoner and guarded by the Yeomen of the Guard, presents purses containing a penny of specially-minted Maundy money for each year of her age, to a group of elderly women and a group of elderly men, who have served their church and community in the area of the Cathedral, each group also to the number of the Queen's age. About £5.50 in ordinary money is also included, in lieu of a clothing provision originally given. Although the gift may seem a token sum, the rarity of the coins gives them a greatly inflated value and they are much sought after by coin dealers, especially coins dating from the beginning of the reign when there were far fewer minted. For example a 1953 set will realize about £140 at auction today.

The origins of this ceremony go back to the thirteenth century when the monarch gave alms and washed the feet of the poor in remembrance of Christ washing the feet of the twelve disciples the night before he was betrayed. James II discontinued the Sovereign's participation in this ceremony, but this was revived by George V in 1932. At this time the Maundy was always distributed at Westminster Abbey, but now the Queen frequently performs the ceremony in cathedrals outside London. Nosegays are carried on this occasion as a reminder that at one time poverty spelt disease, against which a nosegay of potent herbs was supposed to provide, if not immunity, at least some temporary protection.

Although the Lord Steward takes social precedence over the Lord Chamberlain, the department which the Lord Chamberlain controls is of equal importance. It is the department of etiquette and ceremonial or the 'upstairs department'.

Although much more concerned with the day-to-day work of his department than is the Lord Steward, the Lord Chamberlain, at present Lord Maclean, leaves the everyday running of the Lord Chamberlain's Office to the Comptroller, Lt.Col. Sir Eric Penn, and his staff, whose offices are in another part of the Palace. The Lord Chamberlain himself has apartments in St James's Palace. Within his general ambit comes the Ecclesiastical Household, the Central Chancery of the Orders of Knighthood, the Medical Household and the Queen's Bodyguards, although, some of the departments are, in a sense, semi-autonomous. It is the Lord Chamberlain who organizes and arranges, among other things, all Palace ceremonial, incoming state visits, relations with foreign embassies (which is done through the Marshal of the Diplomatic Corps), royal baptisms, weddings and funerals, garden parties and the issue of royal warrants to favoured tradesmen. The line of demarcation between the duties of the Lord Chamberlain and those of the Earl Marshal has always been in dispute, Lord Chamberlains having tended to appropriate more and more of the functions once performed by the heralds under the Earl Marshal, in the days when he was a domestic officer of the Household, rather than a Great Officer of State.

The social if not the equestrian importance of the royal flat race meeting at Ascot is evidenced by the Queen appointing a special representative at Ascot, at present the Marquess of Abergavenny, whose principal business is to vet those who wish to be admitted to the Royal Enclosure and to see that when those so favoured arrive, they are suitable clad. The great draw of Ascot, which was instituted in 1820 by George IV, is the royal procession in 'Ascot Carriages' down the course from the Golden Gates.

My reference to carriages leads naturally to a mention of the third or 'out of doors' department of the Household, that of the Master of the Horse, the Earl of Westmorland. Under his care, or more factually, under the care of his executive officer, the Crown Equerry, comes royal transport, whether it has four legs, or four wheels.

Of the three divisions of the Royal Household only one is presided over by a Great Officer of State and that is the Lord Steward's Department. The Great Officers of State were the equivalent of permanent and often hereditary Cabinet Ministers in the days when Kings ruled as well as reigned. The Lord Steward is the first Great Officer of State, but, as has been seen, his duties are now nominal, unlike those of the second Great Officer, the Lord High Chancellor. He is the head of the judiciary in England and Wales, keeper of the Great Seal of the United Kingdom and prolocutor in the House of Lords, which is very similar to the post of Speaker in the House of Commons. He also has a vast number of other duties and responsibilities.

The Office of Lord High Treasurer, the third Great Officer, is now no more. The national revenue is in the hands of the Treasury, which is nominally controlled by the Commissioners of the defunct office of Lord High Treasurer, headed by the First Lord of the Treasury, who is now usually the Prime Minister. As tax-payers know only too well, the real power in the Treasury is exercised by the Chancellor of the Exchequer.

The other six Great Officers are the Lord President of the Council, the Lord Privy Seal, the Lord Great Chamberlain, the Lord High Constable, the Earl Marshal and the Lord High Admiral. The Earl Marshal's duties have been detailed, the Lord President and Lord Privy Seal and Lord Great Chamberlain have more or less nominal duties; the Lord High Constable is an office now created for the day of a coronation only and the office of Lord High Admiral is now held by the Crown.

Although most of the Great Officers are now little more than ceremonial reminders of the past – historic links with the days when Kings essayed to rule as absolutely as their subjects permitted – paradoxically, he whose power has if anything grown since the Middle Ages – I refer to the Lord Chancellor – is no longer the Sovereign's right-hand man, confidant and secretary as he used to be.

This responsibility of a mediaeval Chancellor is now the care of the Queen's Private Secretary, who is probably the most important of all royal servants. He forms a link with ministers both in the United Kingdom and Commonwealth Countries. He and his assistants deal with all official correspondence, help the Queen to plan her complicated diary, arrange for her personal comfort and tours and official visits, oversee the Press Office and represent her wishes to other departments. It is true to state that however you approach the Queen, your approach will go through her Private Secretary's Office. It is greatly to the credit of this small, but highly efficient, office that all the hundreds of people who write to the Queen daily receive courteous replies and that whenever the Queen performs some official duty, one of the Secretaries will have seen to it personally that the Queen knows exactly what is expected of her, and the body she is honouring also knows exactly what the Queen would like done. Even modest events, such as opening an Old People's Home, predicate a lot of work.

The Secretary in charge must look over the home to assure himself that security arrangements are ad-equate, get in touch with the local police to see that the immediate approaches to the home are kept clear, work out the form which the ceremony will take and arrange which people are to be presented, write up notes on the history of the home so that the Queen can do her 'homework', draft a speech for her consideration, organize transport and then fit everything into a carefully timed programme, leaving a margin for unforseen contingencies. Quite apart from this, the authorities at the home are almost bound to be in a flap, for it is not every day the Queen pays them a visit, which means that from their point of view the occasion will be of historic importance.

They will write innumerable letters and make frantic telephone calls to the Palace – should we do so-and-so? Will the Queen want this or that, or the other? Does she like any special flowers in the bouquet? What if the child presenting it is immobilized with nerves? All these anxieties are alleviated tactfully and confidence is quickly restored by the calm and understanding of the Queen's Secretariat.

Although I have indicated various principal areas of responsibility in the Household, the important point to bear in mind is that these are not now areas of privilege sustaining ancient and archaic prerogatives, but have been tailored to fit the needs of the present day. All departments work together, understanding the chain of command, with the sole, dedicated purpose of serving the Queen so that she may sustain the Crown.

In earlier chapters I have detailed various great ceremonies whose success has been due to the harmony with which the departments of the Household have worked with each other and with Government and other outside agencies.

The Household has to work not only with Government offices, but also with Commonwealth, Colonial and Foreign Governments when the Queen pays official visits abroad. Such visits are very taxing, which is why the Royal Yacht *Britannia* is often used. It is a haven to which the Queen can return, a home in which she can entertain and provides an office for those of the Household who accompany her. The Queen is the most peripatetic monarch Britain has ever had. There is no need to dwell on her innumerable State Visits and tours of the Commonwealth; these have been widely reported and are known to all. I have travelled a little and can bear personal witness that whatever the political climate of any country she has visited, whether it be a foreign nation, or a politically disturbed Commonwealth country, the concensus of opinion after her visit is that Britain could have no better ambassador or the Commonwealth a more beloved Head; on such

occasions anti-monarchists usually retreat to worse positions with their tails very definitely between their legs.

What is important to note is that the Queen has been present constitutionally on a number of occasions in the Commonwealth. In October 1957 she read the Speech from the Throne in the Canadian Parliament at Ottawa, saying 'I greet you as your Queen. Together we constitute the Parliament of Canada'. A few years before she had done the same thing in New Zealand, where she also held three Investitures and attended a meeting of the Privy Council and of the Executive Council, thus emphasizing her royal powers as Queen of New Zealand. In 1974 the Queen of Australia opened Parliament in Canberra. These actions demonstrate the Queen's personal, constitutional relationship with the Member Countries of the Commonwealth. In fact, the Queen's powers are normally exercised vice-regally by Governors-General of Commonwealth countries, Governors in the Colonies and Australian States and Lieutenant-Governors in the Provinces of Canada. Under the terms of the 1931 Statute of Westminster all the Member Countries are 'autonomous communities . . . equal in status, in no way subject to one another in any aspect of their domestic or external affairs, though united by a common allegiance to the Crown and freely associated as the British Commonwealth of Nations'.

It is an imaginative conception, although there are built-in problems, but the symbol of unity is the Crown and the more the Crown can be personalized, the greater the chances of the Commonwealth remaining unfracted.

The Queen is also Supreme Governor of the Church of England. This does not mean that she is endowed with powers over the spiritualities of the Church of England, only over the temporalities. On the advice of the Prime Minister, she appoints Archbishops, Diocesan and Suffregan Bishops, Deans and a number of Canons and incumbents. In the case of appointments of diocesan bishops, the Prime Minister consults the Archbishop of Canterbury and often other noted ecclesiastics of his choice. He then puts the name of the person selected to the Queen. She normally agrees to the appointment, but does not have to; Queen Victoria turned down several persons she considered unsuitable and I doubt whether there would be a constitutional crisis of the Queen followed suit. The name is then sent to the Dean and Chapter of the vacant See with a *congé d'élire* – permission to

The Queen in her study at Balmoral with one of the famous 'red boxes' in which state documents are sent to her.

The Queen and the Duke of Edinburgh at the luncheon in the Guildhall given by the City of London to celebrate their Silver Wedding in 1972.

elect. They then elect the person proposed, there being no legal alternative. The election is confirmed by the Crown's representatives, the new Bishop does homage to the Queen for the temporalities, but not, be it noted, for the spiritualities of his See and is later enthroned in his Cathedral Church. This procedure may seem archaic, but the Church of England is by law established. It is the official religion of the country. The Sovereign must be, and has to swear to be, 'a faithful Protestant' and the Church is represented in the House of Lords as one of the Estates of the Realm. Fortunately, this only applies in England, so the Queen can properly exercise her constitutional functions in other countries of the Commonwealth which have no Protestant Establishment.

It makes the ecclesiastical constitution seem even more tortuous, when it is realized that the Church of Wales is no longer part of the Established Church, having been disestablished at the beginning of the century. To make 'confusion worse confounded' the Queen also has a special relationship with the Church of Scotland, which is a Presbyterian, not a Protestant Episcopalian Church. When the Queen came to the throne she had to sign a declaration that she would maintain the Presbyterian Government of the Church of Scotland, She has secular and temporal, but not spiritual, authority over the Church. Each year the

Opposite: *The Queen and the Duke of Edinburgh at the ceremony of the Opening of Parliament in Australia in Silver Jubilee year, 1977.*

Pages 134–5: *The Queen leading the footguards at the Trooping the Colour ceremony, which celebrates the Queen's Official Birthday.*

Page 136: *The Queen attending the largest children's party ever held, celebrating the International Year of the Child in Hyde Park, London in 1979.*

Page 137: *The Queen opening the General Assembly of the Church of Scotland in the Assembly Hall, Edinburgh in 1969*

Church holds a General Assembly in Edinburgh, presided over by the Moderator of the Church of Scotland 'to legislate and adjudicate finally in all matters of doctrine, worship, government and discipline in the Church'. However, to protect the Queen's secular interests, a Lord High Commissioner is appointed to represent her. This he does in a vice-regal way. For the period of the Assembly he occupies apartments in the Palace of Holyroodhouse and is accorded royal honours.

When the Assembly is opened the High Commissioner walks in procession from St Giles Cathedral to the Assembly Hall, accompanied by Lyon King of Arms. In the Hall he sits apart but delivers a message from the Sovereign to the standing Assembly and is later given a reply to present to Her Majesty. There used to be a dispute as to whether the Assembly convened and dissolved itself or whether this was a Royal Prerogative. The problem has now been amicably settled, the Assembly having been conceded the right of controlling its own affairs. After all, the Queen is not its Governor nor even a member of the Church, so she has no real interest in doing more than the Constitution requires.

Although the Queen does not usually appear in person at the General Assembly she invariably attends the Braemar Gathering in September. This is Highland Games *par excellence* and great fun they are. There are pipe bands, highland dancers and traditional Scottish sports such as chucking two-hundred pounds of pine log – called 'tossing the caber' – over the moon if possible. It is a grand fête and is to Scotland what Royal Ascot is to England; a great national sporting event patronized and really enjoyed by the Sovereign.

There is so much more; so many more things that the Queen does that I can possibly detail and so many more people concerned with the machinery of monarchy than I have indicated. I have called the monarchy a ceremonial monarchy but only in contradistinction to a constitutional monarchy as understood on the Continent of Europe; it is in fact much more. It is a personal, human monarchy which serves the country and the Commonwealth well. The auguries too are good as the Prince of Wales is winning golden opinions and rightly so; the future of the monarchy seems assured. We have been, are and look as if we shall continue to be incredibly lucky in our Head of State, but, and I hope it is not too awful or gloomy to end on a note of admonition, we should be careful not to rely on the personality of the Queen, supported by her family, for the continuity of the monarchy. A true monarchist must support the system as well as the person and one of the surest defences against those who would overthrow the system are, I suggest, the 'predestinate grooves' of our traditional ceremonies.

Bibliography

This is a brief and select bibliography, to supplement such obvious sources as the Encyclopaedia Britannica; the Dictionary of National Biography; *A History of England* (Charles Oman, Ed.) and the *Oxford History of England* (G.N. Clark, Ed.), and other historical works; official ceremonials; the records of ceremonies in the possession of the College of Arms; newspaper reports and accounts of ceremonies in periodicals and a number of diaries and biographies.

BARKER, Brian *The Symbols of Sovereignty* Westbridge Books, 1979

BARKER, Brian *When the Queen was Crowned* Routledge & Kegan Paul, 1976

BENSON, A.C. and Viscount ESHER, Eds. *The Letters of Queen Victoria* John Murray, 1908

BRAY, William, Ed. *The Diary of John Evelyn* Dent, 1907

Burke's Guide to the Royal Family, Burke's Peerage, 1973

CLARK, Brig. Stanley *Palace Diary* Harrap, 1958

CONNIHAN, Daniel *Royal Progress* Cassell, 1977

DERRIMAN, James *Pageantry of the Law* Eyre and Spottiswoode, 1955

'EUPHAN and KLAXON' *Stories of the Coronation* Burns, Oates and Washbourne, 1937

FLETCHER, I.K. *The British Court* Cassell, 1953

GORE, John *King George V* John Murray 1941

HOLMES, Martin and SITWELL, Maj-Gen. H.D.W. *The English Regalia* H.M.S.O., 1972

JONES, Francis *The Princes and Principality of Wales* U. of Wales Press, 1969

LACY, Robert *Majesty* Hutchinson, 1977

LAIRD, Dorothy *How the Queen Reigns* Hodder & Stoughton, 1959

MACLEANE, Douglas *The Great Solemnity of the Coronation* George Allen, 1911

MAGNUS, Philip *King Edward VII* John Murray, 1964

MILTON, Roger *The English Ceremonial Book* David & Charles, 1972

MORRIS, Canon Rupert H. *The Investiture of the Prince of Wales* Archeologia Cambrensis, 6th Series, vol 2, 1911

ROUND, J. Horace *The King's Serjeants and Officers of State* James Nesbit, 1911

SITWELL, Maj-Gen. H.D.W. *The Crown Jewels* Dropmore Press, 1953

STUBBS, William *The Constitutional History of England* Clarendon Press, 1891

TANNER, Lawrence E. *The History of the Coronation* Pitkin, 1952

TURNER, E.S. *At The Court of St. James's* Michael Joseph, 1959

UDEN, Grant *A Dictionary of Chivalry* Longman, 1968

WADE, E.S.C. and BRADLEY, A.W. *Constitutional Law* Michael Joseph, 1960

WAGNER, Sir Anthony *Heralds of England* H.M.S.O., 1967

WAGNER, Sir Anthony and SAINTY, J.O. *The Origin of the Introduction of Peers into the House of Lords* Archeologia, vol CI, 1967

WINDSOR, H.R.H. the Duke of (Memoirs) *A King's Story* Cassell, 1951

WOLLASTON, Sir Gerald *The Court of Claims* Harrison, 1903

Picture Acknowledgements and List of Colour Plates

Permission to reproduce photographs has kindly been given by the following; for easy reference, page numbers in bold refer to colour illustrations.

Graphische Sammlung Albertina: 24. The British Library: 17 (Stowe MS 594), 66–7 (Add. MS 22306), 98 (Stowe MS 594). Central Press Photos: 78. The College of Arms: **18, 22, 23, 26, 35, 48, 50, 51** (above), 52, 77, 106, **107**, 110. Fox Photos: 11, 32, **53, 54**, 60, **71**, 74, **89, 90, 91, 92**, 101, 103, 112, 114, 121, 122, 125, 126–7, 130, 132, **136, 137**. Michael Franks: 13. Keystone Press Agency: 25. Mansell Collection: 28, 34, 38–9, 40 (both), 82, 117, 119. Courtesy of National Film Archive/Stills Library: 56–7. National Gallery: 14. National Portrait Gallery: 83. The order of St John: 96, 97. Pitkin Pictorials: **108**. Press Association: 30. Radio Times Hulton Picture Library: 16, 21, 42, 45, 46, 51 (below), 63, 88, 109, 120. Royal Library, Windsor Castle, reproduced by Gracious Permission of Her Majesty The Queen: 86. John Scott: **36, 72, 133, 134–5**. Universal Pictorial Press: 68.

Index